SPALDING'S
ATHLETIC LIBRARY

WATER POLO

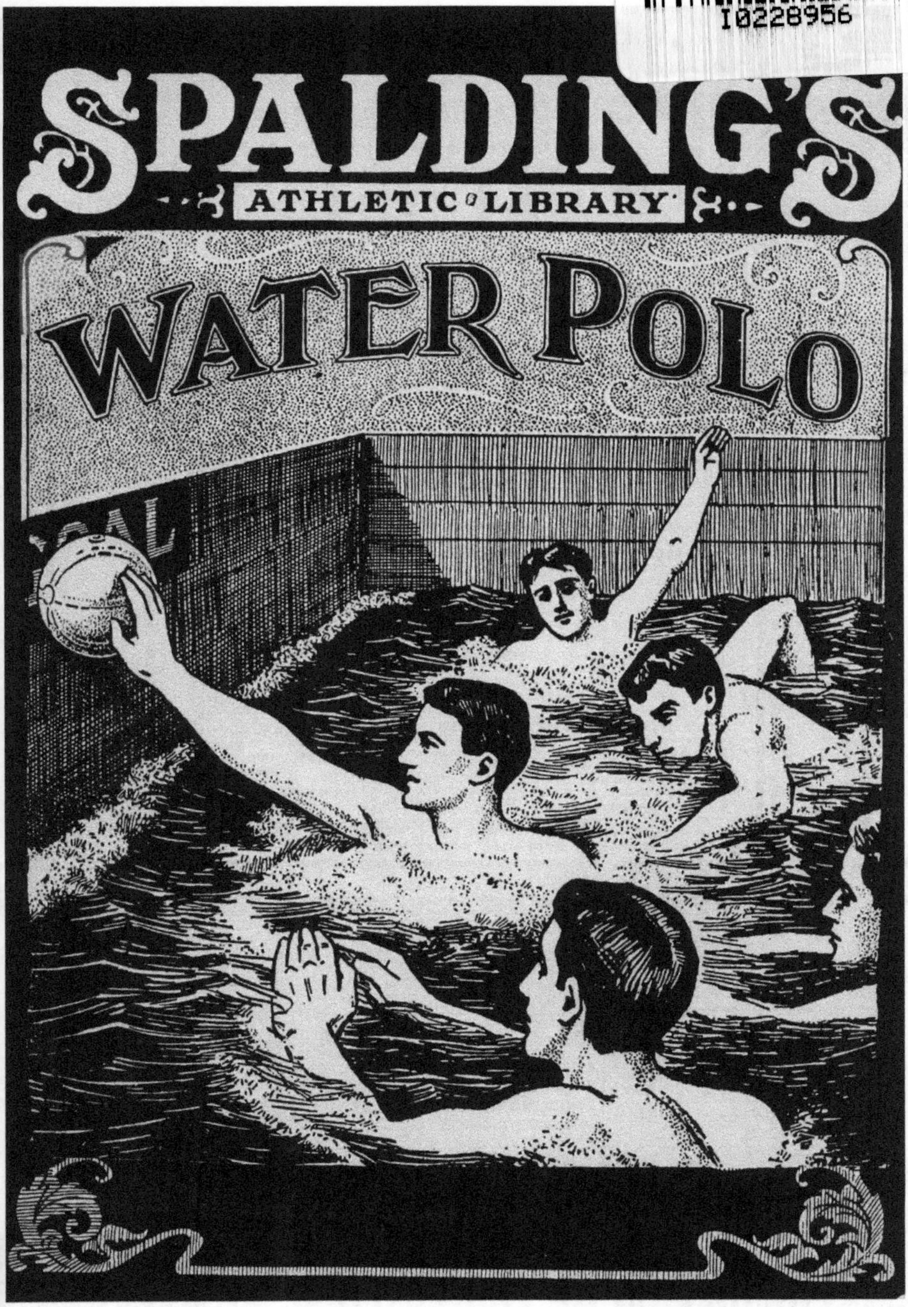

Spalding's Athletic Library

A. G. SPALDING

Anticipating the present tendency of the American people toward a healthful method of living and enjoyment, Spalding's Athletic Library was established in 1892 for the purpose of encouraging athletics in every form, not only by publishing the official rules and records pertaining to the various pastimes, but also by instructing, until to-day Spalding's Athletic Library is unique in its own particular field and has been conceded the greatest educational series on athletic and physical training subjects that has ever been compiled.

The publication of a distinct series of books devoted to athletic sports and pastimes and designed to occupy the premier place in America in its class was an early idea of Mr. A. G. Spalding, who was one of the first in America to publish a handbook devoted to athletic sports, Spalding's Official Base Ball Guide being the initial number, which was followed at intervals with other handbooks on the sports prominent in the '70s.

Spalding's Athletic Library has had the advice and counsel of Mr. A. G. Spalding in all of its undertakings, and particularly in all books devoted to the national game. This applies especially to Spalding's Official Base Ball Guide and Spalding's Official Base Ball Record, both of which receive the personal attention of Mr. A. G. Spalding, owing to his early connection with the game as the leading pitcher of the champion Boston and Chicago teams of 1872-76. His interest does not stop, however, with matters pertaining to base ball; there is not a sport that Mr. Spalding does not make it his business to become familiar with, and that the Library will always maintain its premier place, with Mr. Spalding's able counsel at hand, goes without saying.

The entire series since the issue of the first number has been under the direct personal supervision of Mr. James E. Sullivan, President of the American Sports Publishing Company, and the total series of consecutive numbers reach an aggregate of considerably over three hundred, included in which are many "annuals," that really constitute the history of their particular sport in America year by year, back copies of which are even now eagerly sought for, constituting as they do the really first authentic records of events and official rules that have ever been consecutively compiled.

When Spalding's Athletic Library was founded, seventeen years ago, track and field athletics were practically unknown outside the larger colleges and a few athletic clubs in the leading cities, which gave occasional meets, when an entry list of 250 competitors was a subject of comment; golf was known only by a comparatively few persons; lawn tennis had some vogue and base ball was practically the only established field

EDITORS OF SPALDING'S ATHLETIC LIBRARY

sport, and that in a professional way; basket ball had just been invented; athletics for the schoolboy—and schoolgirl—were almost unknown, and an advocate of class contests in athletics in the schools could not get a hearing. To-day we find the greatest body of athletes in the world is the Public Schools Athletic League of Greater New York, which has had an entry list at its annual games of over two thousand, and in whose "elementary series" in base ball last year 106 schools competed for the trophy emblematic of the championship.

While Spalding's Athletic Library cannot claim that the rapid growth of athletics in this country is due to it solely, the fact cannot be denied that the books have had a great deal to do with its encouragement, by printing the official rules and instructions for playing the various games at a nominal price, within the reach of everyone, with the sole object that its series might be complete and the one place where a person could look with absolute certainty for the particular book in which he might be interested.

In selecting the editors and writers for the various books, the leading authority in his particular line has been obtained, with the result that no collection of books on athletic subjects can compare with Spalding's Athletic Library for the prominence of the various authors and their ability to present their subjects in a thorough and practical manner.

A short sketch of a few of those who have edited some of the leading numbers of Spalding's Athletic Library is given herewith:

JAMES E. SULLIVAN

President American Sports Publishing Company; entered the publishing house of Frank Leslie in 1878, and has been connected continuously with the publishing business since then and also as athletic editor of various New York papers; was a competing athlete; one of the organizers of the Amateur Athletic Union of the United States; has been actively on its board of governors since its organization until the present time, and President for two successive terms; has attended every championship meeting in America since 1879 and has officiated in some capacity in connection with American amateur championships track and field games for nearly twenty-five years; assistant American director Olympic Games, Paris, 1900; director Pan-American Exposition athletic department, 1901; chief department physical culture Louisiana Purchase Exposition, St. Louis, 1904; secretary American Committee Olympic Games, at Athens, 1906; honorary director of Athletics at Jamestown Exposition, 1907; secretary American Committee Olympic Games, at London, 1908; member of the Pastime A. C., New York: honorary member Missouri A. C., St. Louis; honorary member Olympic A. C., San Francisco; ex-president Pastime A. C., New Jersey A. C., Knickerbocker A. C.; president Metropolitan Association of the A. A. U. for fifteen years; president Outdoor Recreation League; with Dr. Luther H. Gulick organized the Public Schools Athletic League of New York, and is now chairman of its games committee and member executive committee; was a pioneer in playground work and one of the organizers of the Outdoor Recreation League of New York; appointed by President Roosevelt as special commissioner to the Olympic Games at Athens, 1906, and decorated by King George I. of the Hellenes (Greece) for his services in connection with the Olympic Games; appointed special commissioner by President Roosevelt to the Olympic Games at London, 1908; appointed by Mayor McClellan, 1908, as member of the Board of Education of Greater New York.

EDITORS OF SPALDING'S ATHLETIC LIBRARY

WALTER CAMP

For quarter of a century Mr. Walter Camp of Yale has occupied a leading position in college athletics. It is immaterial what organization is suggested for college athletics, or for the betterment of conditions, insofar as college athletics is concerned. Mr. Camp has always played an important part in its conferences, and the great interest in and high plane of college sport to-day, are undoubtedly due more to Mr. Camp than to any other individual. Mr. Camp has probably written more on college athletics than any other writer and the leading papers and magazines of America are always anxious to secure his expert opinion on foot ball, track and field athletics, base ball and rowing. Mr. Camp has grown up with Yale athletics and is a part of Yale's remarkable athletic system. While he has been designated as the "Father of Foot Ball," it is a well known fact that during his college career Mr. Camp was regarded as one of the best players that ever represented Yale on the base ball field, so when we hear of Walter Camp as a foot ball expert we must also remember his remarkable knowledge of the game of base ball, of which he is a great admirer. Mr. Camp has edited Spalding's Official Foot Ball Guide since it was first published, and also the Spalding Athletic Library book on How to Play Foot Ball. There is certainly no man in American college life better qualified to write for Spalding's Athletic Library than Mr. Camp.

DR. LUTHER HALSEY GULICK

The leading exponent of physical training in America; one who has worked hard to impress the value of physical training in the schools; when physical training was combined with education at the St. Louis Exposition in 1904 Dr. Gulick played an important part in that congress; he received several awards for his good work and had many honors conferred upon him; he is the author of a great many books on the subject; it was Dr. Gulick, who, acting on the suggestion of James E. Sullivan, organized the Public Schools Athletic League of Greater New York, and was its first Secretary; Dr. Gulick was also for several years Director of Physical Training in the public schools of Greater New York, resigning the position to assume the Presidency of the Playground Association of America. Dr. Gulick is an authority on all subjects pertaining to physical training and the study of the child.

JOHN B. FOSTER

Successor to the late Henry Chadwick ("Father of Base Ball") as editor of Spalding's Official Base Ball Guide; sporting editor of the New York Evening Telegram; has been in the newspaper business for many years and is recognized throughout America as a leading writer on the national game; a staunch supporter of organized base ball, his pen has always been used for the betterment of the game.

EDITORS OF SPALDING'S ATHLETIC LIBRARY

TIM MURNANE
Base Ball editor of the Boston Globe and President of the New England League of Base Ball Clubs; one of the best known base ball men of the country; known from coast to coast; is a keen follower of the game and prominent in all its councils; nearly half a century ago was one of America's foremost players; knows the game thoroughly and writes from the point of view both of player and an official.

HARRY PHILIP BURCHELL
Sporting editor of the New York Times; graduate of the University of Pennsylvania; editor of Spalding's Official Lawn Tennis Annual; is an authority on the game; follows the movements of the players minutely and understands not only tennis but all other subjects that can be classed as athletics; no one is better qualified to edit this book than Mr. Burchell.

GEORGE T. HEPBRON
Former Young Men's Christian Association director; for many years an official of the Athletic League of Young Men's Christian Associations of North America; was connected with Dr. Luther H. Gulick in Young Men's Christian Association work for over twelve years; became identified with basket ball when it was in its infancy and has followed it since, being recognized as the leading exponent of the official rules; succeeded Dr. Gulick as editor of the Official Basket Ball Guide and also editor of the Spalding Athletic Library book on How to Play Basket Ball.

JAMES S. MITCHEL
Former champion weight thrower; holder of numerous records, and is the winner of more championships than any other individual in the history of sport; Mr. Mitchel is a close student of athletics and well qualified to write upon any topic connected with athletic sport; has been for years on the staff of the New York Sun.

EDITORS OF SPALDING'S ATHLETIC LIBRARY

MICHAEL C MURPHY

The world's most famous athletic trainer; the champion athletes that he has developed for track and field sports, foot ball and base ball fields, would run into thousands; he became famous when at Yale University and has been particularly successful in developing what might be termed championship teams; his rare good judgment has placed him in an enviable position in the athletic world; now with the University of Pennsylvania; during his career has trained only at two colleges and one athletic club, Yale and the University of Pennsylvania and Detroit Athletic Club; his most recent triumph was that of training the famous American team of athletes that swept the field at the Olympic Games of 1908 at London.

DR. C. WARD CRAMPTON

Succeeded Dr. Gulick as director of physical training in the schools of Greater New York; as secretary of the Public Schools Athletic League is at the head of the most remarkable organization of its kind in the world; is a practical athlete and gymnast himself, and has been for years connected with the physical training system in the schools of Greater New York, having had charge of the High School of Commerce.

DR. GEORGE J. FISHER

Has been connected with Y. M. C. A. work for many years as physical director at Cincinnati and Brooklyn, where he made such a high reputation as organizer that he was chosen to succeed Dr. Luther H. Gulick as Secretary of the Athletic League of Y. M. C. A.'s of North America, when the latter resigned to take charge of the physical training in the Public Schools of Greater New York.

DR. GEORGE ORTON

On athletics, college athletics, particularly track and field, foot ball, soccer foot ball, and training of the youth, it would be hard to find one better qualified than Dr. Orton; has had the necessary athletic experience and the ability to impart that experience intelligently to the youth of the land; for years was the American, British and Canadian champion runner.

EDITORS OF SPALDING'S ATHLETIC LIBRARY

FREDERICK R. TOOMBS
A well known authority on skating, rowing, boxing, racquets, and other athletic sports; was sporting editor of American Press Association, New York; dramatic editor; is a lawyer and has served several terms as a member of Assembly of the Legislature of the State of New York; has written several novels and historical works.

R. L. WELCH
A resident of Chicago; the popularity of indoor base ball is chiefly due to his efforts; a player himself of no mean ability; a first-class organizer; he has followed the game of indoor base ball from its inception.

DR. HENRY S. ANDERSON
Has been connected with Yale University for years and is a recognized authority on gymnastics; is admitted to be one of the leading authorities in America on gymnastic subjects; is the author of many books on physical training.

CHARLES M. DANIELS
Just the man to write an authoritative book on swimming; the fastest swimmer the world has ever known; member New York Athletic Club swimming team and an Olympic champion at Athens in 1906 and London, 1908. In his book on Swimming, Champion Daniels describes just the methods one must use to become an expert swimmer.

GUSTAVE BOJUS
Mr. Bojus is most thoroughly qualified to write intelligently on all subjects pertaining to gymnastics and athletics; in his day one of America's most famous amateur athletes; has competed successfully in gymnastics and many other sports for the New York Turn Verein; for twenty years he has been prominent in teaching gymnastics and athletics; was responsible for the famous gymnastic championship teams of Columbia University; now with the Jersey City high schools.

EDITORS OF SPALDING'S ATHLETIC LIBRARY

CHARLES JACOBUS
Admitted to be the "Father of Roque;" one of America's most expert players, winning the Olympic Championship at St. Louis in 1904; an ardent supporter of the game and follows it minutely, and much of the success of roque is due to his untiring efforts; certainly there is no one better qualified to write on this subject than Mr. Jacobus.

DR. E. B. WARMAN
Well known as a physical training expert; was probably one of the first to enter the field and is the author of many books on the subject; lectures extensively each year all over the country.

W. J. CROMIE
Now with the University of Pennsylvania; was formerly a Y. M. C. A. physical director; a keen student of all gymnastic matters; the author of many books on subjects pertaining to physical training.

G. M. MARTIN
By profession a physical director of the Young Men's Christian Association; a close student of all things gymnastic, and games for the classes in the gymnasium or clubs.

PROF. SENAC
A leader in the fencing world; has maintained a fencing school in New York for years and developed a great many champions; understands the science of fencing thoroughly and the benefits to be derived therefrom.

SPALDING ATHLETIC LIBRARY

Giving the Titles of all Spalding Athletic Library Books now in print, grouped for ready reference

SPALDING OFFICIAL ANNUALS

No. 1 Spalding's Official Base Ball Guide
No. 1A Spalding's Official Base Ball Record
No. 2 Spalding's Official Foot Ball Guide
No. 2A Spalding's Official Soccer Foot Ball Guide
No. 3 Spalding's Official Cricket Guide
No. 4 Spalding's Official Lawn Tennis Annual
No. 5 Spalding's Official Golf Guide
No. 6 Spalding's Official Ice Hockey Guide
No. 7 Spalding's Official Basket Ball Guide
No. 8 Spalding's Official Bowling Guide
No. 9 Spalding's Official Indoor Base Ball Guide
No. 10 Spalding's Official Roller Polo Guide
No. 12 Spalding's Official Athletic Almanac

Group I. Base Ball
No. 1 *Spalding's Official Base Ball Guide.*
No. 1A Official Base Ball Record.
No. 202 How to Play Base Ball.
No. 223 How to Bat.
No. 232 How to Run Bases.
No. 230 How to Pitch.
No. 229 How to Catch.
No. 225 How to Play First Base.
No. 226 How to Play Second Base.
No. 227 How to Play Third Base.
No. 228 How to Play Shortstop.
No. 224 How to Play the Outfield.
No. 231 {How to Organize a Base Ball Club. [League.
How to Organize a Base Ball
How to Manage a Base Ball Club.
How to Train a Base Ball Team
How to Captain a Base Ball
How to Umpire a Game. [Team
Technical Base Ball Terms.
No. 219 Ready Reckoner of Base Ball Percentages.

BASE BALL AUXILIARIES
No. 319 Minor League Base Ball Guide
No. 320 Official Book National League of Prof. Base Ball Clubs.
No. 321 Official Handbook National Playground Ball Assn.

Group II. Foot Ball
No. 2 *Spalding's Official Foot Ball Guide.*
No. 334 Code of the Foot Ball Rules.
No. 324 How to Play Foot Ball.
No. 2A *Spalding's Official Soccer Foot Ball Guide.*
No. 286 How to Play Soccer.

FOOT BALL AUXILIARY
No. 332 Spalding's Official Canadian Foot Ball Guide.
No. 335 Spalding's Official Rugby Foot Ball Guide.

Group III. Cricket
No. 3 *Spalding's Official Cricket Guide.*
No. 277 Cricket and How to Play It.

Group IV. Lawn Tennis
No. 4 *Spalding's Official Lawn Tennis Annual.*
No. 157 How to Play Lawn Tennis.
No. 279 Strokes and Science of Lawn Tennis.

Group V. Golf
No. 5 *Spalding's Official Golf Guide.*
No. 276 How to Play Golf.

Group VI. Hockey
No. 6 *Spalding's Official Ice Hockey Guide.*
No. 304 How to Play Ice Hockey.
No. 154 Field Hockey.
No. 188 {Lawn Hockey. Parlor Hockey. Garden Hockey.
No. 180 Ring Hockey.

HOCKEY AUXILIARY
No. 256 Official Handbook Ontario Hockey Association.

Group VII. Basket Ball
No. 7 *Spalding's Official Basket Ball Guide.*
No. 193 How to Play Basket Ball.
No. 318 Basket Ball Guide for Women.

BASKET BALL AUXILIARY
No. 323 Official Collegiate Basket Ball Handbook.

ANY OF THE ABOVE BOOKS MAILED POSTPAID UPON RECEIPT OF 10 CENTS

SPALDING ATHLETIC LIBRARY

Group VIII. Bowling
No. 8 *Spalding's Official Bowling Guide.*

Group IX. Indoor Base Ball
No. 9 *Spalding's Official Indoor Base Ball Guide.*

Group X. Polo
No. 10 *Spalding's Official Roller Polo Guide.*
No. 129 Water Polo.
No. 199 Equestrian Polo.

Group XI. Miscellaneous Games
No. 201 Lacrosse.
No. 322 Official Handbook U. S. Intercollegiate Lacrosse League.
No. 248 Archery.
No. 138 Croquet.
No. 271 Roque.
No. 194 {Racquets. Squash-Racquets. Court Tennis.
No. 13 Hand Ball.
No. 167 Quoits.
No. 170 Push Ball.
No. 14 Curling.
No. 207 Lawn Bowls.
No. 188 Lawn Games.
No. 189 Children's Games.

Group XII. Athletics
No. 12 *Spalding's Official Athletic Almanac.*
No. 27 College Athletics.
No. 182 All Around Athletics.
No. 156 Athletes' Guide.
No. 87 Athletic Primer.
No. 273 Olympic Games at Athens, 1906
No. 252 How to Sprint.
No. 255 How to Run 100 Yards.
No. 174 Distance and Cross Country Running. [Thrower.
No. 259 How to Become a Weight
No. 55 Official Sporting Rules. [boys.
No. 246 Athletic Training for School-
No. 317 Marathon Running.
No. 331 Schoolyard Athletics.

ATHLETIC AUXILIARIES
No. 311 Amateur Athletic Union Official Handbook. [book.
No. 316 Intercollegiate Official Handbook.
No. 302 Y. M. C. A. Official Handbook.
No. 313 Public Schools Athletic League Official Handbook.
No. 314 Public Schools Athletic League Official Handbook—Girls' Branch.
No. 308 Official Handbook New York Interscholastic Athletic Association.

Group XIII. Athletic Accomplishments
No. 177 How to Swim.
No. 296 Speed Swimming.
No. 128 How to Row.
No. 209 How to Become a Skater.
No. 178 How to Train for Bicycling.
No. 23 Canoeing.
No. 282 Roller Skating Guide.

Group XIV. Manly Sports
No. 18 Fencing. (By Breck.)
No. 162 Boxing.
No. 165 Fencing. (By Senac.)
No. 140 Wrestling.
No. 236 How to Wrestle.
No. 102 Ground Tumbling.
No. 233 Jiu Jitsu.
No. 166 How to Swing Indian Clubs.
No. 200 Dumb Bell Exercises.
No. 143 Indian Clubs and Dumb Bells.
No. 262 Medicine Ball Exercises.
No. 29 Pulley Weight Exercises.
No. 191 How to Punch the Bag.
No. 289 Tumbling for Amateurs.
No. 326 Professional Wrestling.

Group XV. Gymnastics
No. 104 Grading of Gymnastic Exercises. [Dumb Bell Drills.
No. 214 Graded Calisthenics and
No. 254 Barnjum Bar Bell Drill.
No. 158 Indoor and Outdoor Gymnastic Games.
No. 124 How to Become a Gymnast.
No. 287 Fancy Dumb Bell and Marching Drills. [Apparatus.
No. 327 Pyramid Building Without
No. 328 Exercises on the Parallel Bars.
No. 329 Pyramid Building with Wands, Chairs and Ladders
GYMNASTIC AUXILIARY
No. 333 Official Handbook I. C. A. A. Gymnasts of America.

Group XVI. Physical Culture
No. 161 Ten Minutes' Exercise for Busy Men. [giene.
No. 208 Physical Education and Hygiene.
No. 149 Scientific Physical Training and Care of the Body.
No. 142 Physical Training Simplified.
No. 185 Hints on Health.
No. 213 285 Health Answers.
No. 238 Muscle Building. [ning.
No. 234 School Tactics and Maze Running.
No. 261 Tensing Exercises. [nastics.
No. 285 Health by Muscular Gymnastics.
No. 288 Indigestion Treated by Gymnastics.
No. 290 Get Well; Keep Well. [nastics.
No. 325 Twenty-Minute Exercises.
No. 330 Physical Training for the School and Class Room.

ANY OF THE ABOVE BOOKS MAILED POSTPAID UPON RECEIPT OF 10 CENTS

SPALDING ATHLETIC LIBRARY

Group I. Base Ball

No. 1—Spalding's Official Base Ball Guide.

The leading Base Ball annual of the country, and the official authority of the game. Contains the official playing rules, with an explanatory index of the rules compiled by Mr. A. G. Spalding; pictures of all the teams in the National, American and minor leagues; reviews of the season; college Base Ball, and a great deal of interesting information. Price 10 cents.

No. 1A — Spalding's Official Base Ball Record.

Something new in Base Ball. Contains records of all kinds from the beginning of the National League and official averages of all professional organizations for past season. Illustrated with pictures of leading teams and players. Price 10 cents.

No. 202—How to Play Base Ball.

Edited by Tim Murnane. New and revised edition. Illustrated with pictures showing how all the various curves and drops are thrown and portraits of leading players. Price 10 cents.

No. 223—How to Bat.

There is no better way of becoming a proficient batter than by reading this book and practising the directions. Numerous illustrations. Price 10 cents.

No. 232—How to Run the Bases.

This book gives clear and concise directions for excelling as a base runner; tells when to run and when not to do so; how and when to slide; team work on the bases; in fact, every point of the game is thoroughly explained. Illustrated. Price 10 cents.

No. 230—How to Pitch.

A new, up-to-date book. Its contents are the practical teaching of men who have reached the top as pitchers, and who know how to impart a knowledge of their art. All the big leagues' pitchers are shown. Price 10 cents.

No. 229—How to Catch.

Every boy who has hopes of being a clever catcher should read how well-known players cover their position. Pictures of all the noted catchers in the big leagues. Price 10 cents.

No. 225—How to Play First Base.

Illustrated with pictures of all the prominent first basemen. Price 10 cents.

No. 226—How to Play Second Base.

The ideas of the best second basemen have been incorporated in this book for the especial benefit of boys who want to know the fine points of play at this point of the diamond. Price 10 cents.

No. 227—How to Play Third Base.

Third base is, in some respects, the most important of the infield. All the points explained. Price 10 cents.

No. 228—How to Play Shortstop.

Shortstop is one of the hardest positions on the infield to fill, and quick thought and quick action are necessary for a player who expects to make good as a shortstop. Illus. Price 10 cents.

No. 224—How to Play the Outfield.

An invaluable guide for the outfielder. Price 10 cents.

No. 231—How to Coach; How to Captain a Team; How to Manage a Team; How to Umpire; How to Organize a League; Technical Terms of Base Ball.

A useful guide. Price 10 cents.

No. 219—Ready Reckoner of Base Ball Percentages.

To supply a demand for a book which would show the percentage of clubs without recourse to the arduous work of figuring, the publishers had these tables compiled by an expert. Price 10 cents.

BASE BALL AUXILIARIES.

No. 319—Minor League Base Ball Guide.

The minors' own guide. Edited by President T. H. Murnane, of the New England League. Price 10 cents.

SPALDING ATHLETIC LIBRARY

No. 320—Official Handbook of the National League of Professional Base Ball Clubs.

Contains the Constitution, By-Laws, Official Rules, Averages, and schedule of the National League for the current year, together with list of club officers and reports of the annual meetings of the League. Price 10 cents.

No. 321—Official Handbook National Playground Ball Association.

This game is specially adapted for playgrounds, parks, etc., is spreading rapidly. The book contains a description of the game, rules and list of officers. Price 10 cents.

Group II. Foot Ball

No. 2—Spalding's Official Foot Ball Guide.

Edited by Walter Camp. Contains the new rules, with diagram of field; All-America teams as selected by the leading authorities; reviews of the game from various sections of the country; scores; pictures. Price 10 cents.

No. 334—Code of the Foot Ball Rules.

This book is meant for the use of officials, to help them to refresh their memories before a game and to afford them a quick means of ascertaining a point during a game. It also gives a ready means of finding a rule in the Official Rule Book, and is of great help to a player in studying the Rules. Compiled by C. W. Short, Harvard, 1908. Price 10 cents.

No. 324—How to Play Foot Ball.

Edited by Walter Camp, of Yale. Everything that a beginner wants to know and many points that an expert will be glad to learn. Snapshots of leading teams and players in action, with comments by Walter Camp. Price 10 cents.

No. 2A—Spalding's Official Association Soccer Foot Ball Guide.

A complete and up-to-date guide to the "Soccer" game in the United States, containing instructions for playing the game, official rules, and interesting news from all parts of the country. Illustrated. Price 10 cents.

No. 286—How to Play Soccer.

How each position should be played, written by the best player in England in his respective position, and illustrated with full-page photographs of players in action. Price 10 cents.

FOOT BALL AUXILIARIES.

No. 332—Spalding's Official Canadian Foot Ball Guide.

The official book of the game in Canada. Price 10 cents.

No. 335—Spalding's Official Rugby Foot Ball Guide.

Contains the official rules under which the game is played in England and by the California schools and colleges. Also instructions for playing the various positions on a team. Illustrated with action pictures of leading teams and players. Price 10 cents.

Group III. Cricket

No. 3—Spalding's Official Cricket Guide.

The most complete year book of the game that has ever been published in America. Reports of special matches, official rules and pictures of all the leading teams. Price 10 cents.

No. 277—Cricket; and How to Play it.

By Prince Ranjitsinhji. The game described concisely and illustrated with full-page pictures posed especially for this book. Price 10 cents.

SPALDING ATHLETIC LIBRARY

Group IV. Lawn Tennis

No. 4—Spalding's Official Lawn Tennis Annual.

Contents include reports of all important tournaments; official ranking from 1885 to date; laws of lawn tennis; instructions for handicapping; decisions on doubtful points; management of tournaments; directory of clubs; laying out and keeping a court. Illustrated. Price 10 cents.

No. 157—How to Play Lawn Tennis.

A complete description of lawn tennis; a lesson for beginners and directions telling how to make the most important strokes. Illustrated. Price 10 cents.

No. 279—Strokes and Science of Lawn Tennis.

By P. A. Vaile, a leading authority on the game in Great Britain. Every stroke in the game is accurately illustrated and analyzed by the author. Price 10 cents.

Group V. Golf

No. 5—Spalding's Official Golf Guide.

Contains records of all important tournaments, articles on the game in various sections of the country, pictures of prominent players, official playing rules and general items of interest. Price 10 cents.

No. 276—How to Play Golf.

By James Braid and Harry Vardon, the world's two greatest players tell how they play the game, with numerous full-page pictures of them taken on the links. Price 10 cents.

Group VI. Hockey

No. 6—Spalding's Official Ice Hockey Guide.

The official year book of the game. Contains the official rules, pictures of leading teams and players, records, review of the season, reports from different sections of the United States and Canada. Price 10 cents.

No. 304—How to Play Ice Hockey.

Contains a description of the duties of each player. Illustrated. Price 10 cents.

No. 154—Field Hockey.

Prominent in the sports at Vassar, Smith, Wellesley, Bryn Mawr and other leading colleges. Price 10 cents.

No. 188—Lawn Hockey, Parlor Hockey, Garden Hockey.

Containing the rules for each game. Illustrated. Price 10 cents.

No. 180—Ring Hockey.

A new game for the gymnasium. Exciting as basket ball. Price 10 cents.

HOCKEY AUXILIARY.

No. 256—Official Handbook of the Ontario Hockey Association.

Contains the official rules of the Association, constitution, rules of competition, list of officers, and pictures of leading players. Price 10 cents.

Group VII. Basket Ball

No. 7—Spalding's Official Basket Ball Guide.

Edited by George T. Hepbron. Contains the revised official rules, decisions on disputed points, records of prominent teams, reports on the game from various parts of the country. Illustrated. Price 10 cents.

SPALDING ATHLETIC LIBRARY

No. 193—How to Play Basket Ball.

By G. T. Hepbron, editor of the Official Basket Ball Guide. Illustrated with scenes of action. Price 10 cents.

No. 318—Official Basket Ball Guide for Women.

Edited by Miss Senda Berenson, of Smith College. Contains the official playing rules and special articles on the game by prominent authorities. Illustrated. Price 10 cents.

BASKET BALL AUXILIARY.

No. 323—Collegiate Basket Ball Handbook.

The official publication of the Collegiate Basket Ball Association. Contains the official rules, records, All-America selections, reviews, and pictures. Edited by H. A. Fisher, of Columbia. Price 10 cents.

Group VIII. Bowling

No. 8—Spalding's Official Bowling Guide.

The contents include: diagrams of effective deliveries; hints to beginners; how to score; official rules; spares, how they are made; rules for cocked hat, quintet, cocked hat and feather, battle game, etc. Price 10 cents.

Group IX. Indoor Base Ball

No. 9—Spalding's Official Indoor Base Ball Guide.

America's national game is now vieing with other indoor games as a winter pastime. This book contains the playing rules, pictures of leading teams, and interesting articles on the game by leading authorities on the subject. Price 10 cents.

Group X.   Polo

No. 10—Spalding's Official Roller Polo Guide.

Edited by J. C. Morse. A full description of the game; official rules, records; pictures of prominent players. Price 10 cents.

No. 129—Water Polo.

The contents of this book treat of every detail, the individual work of the players, the practice of the team, how to throw the ball, with illustrations and many valuable hints. Price 10 cents.

No. 199—Equestrian Polo.

Compiled by H. L. Fitzpatrick of the New York Sun. Illustrated with portraits of leading players, and contains most useful information for polo players. Price 10 cents.

Group XI. Miscellaneous Games

No. 201—Lacrosse.

Every position is thoroughly explained in a most simple and concise manner, rendering it the best manual of the game ever published. Illustrated with numerous snapshots of important plays. Price 10 cents.

No. 322—Official Handbook U. S. Inter-Collegiate Lacrosse League.

Contains the constitution, by-laws, playing rules, list of officers and records of the association. Price 10 cents.

No. 271—Spalding's Official Roque Guide.

The official publication of the National Roque Association of America. Contains a description of the courts and their construction, diagrams, illustrations, rules and valuable information. Price 10 cents.

SPALDING ATHLETIC LIBRARY

No. 138—Spalding's Official Croquet Guide

Contains directions for playing, diagrams of important strokes, description of grounds, instructions for the beginner, terms used in the game, and the official playing rules. Price 10 cents.

No. 248—Archery.

A new and up-to-date book on this fascinating pastime. The several varieties of archery; instructions for shooting; how to select implements; how to score; and a great deal of interesting information. Illustrated. Price 10 cents.

No. 194—Racquets, Squash-Racquets and Court Tennis.

How to play each game is thoroughly explained, and all the difficult strokes shown by special photographs taken especially for this book. Contains the official rules for each game. Price 10 cents.

No. 167—Quoits.

Contains a description of the plays used by experts and the official rules. Illustrated. Price 10 cents.

No. 170—Push Ball.

This book contains the official rules and a sketch of the game; illustrated. Price 10 cents.

No. 13—How to Play Hand Ball.

By the world's champion, Michael Egan. Every play is thoroughly explained by text and diagram. Illustrated. Price 10 cents.

No. 14—Curling.

A short history of this famous Scottish pastime, with instructions for play, rules of the game, definitions of terms and diagrams of different shots. Price 10 cents.

No. 207—Bowling on the Green; or, Lawn Bowls.

How to construct a green; how to play the game, and the official rules of the Scottish Bowling Association. Illustrated. Price 10 cents.

No. 189—Children's Games.

These games are intended for use at recesses, and all but the team games have been adapted to large classes. Suitable for children from three to eight years, and include a great variety. Price 10 cents.

No. 188—Lawn Games.

Lawn Hockey, Garden Hockey, Hand Tennis, Tether Tennis; also Volley Ball, Parlor Hockey, Badminton, Basket Goal. Price 10 cents.

Group XII. Athletics

No. 12—Spalding's Official Athletic Almanac.

Compiled by J. E. Sullivan, President of the Amateur Athletic Union. The only annual publication now issued that contains a complete list of amateur best-on-records; intercollegiate, swimming, interscholastic, English, Irish, Scotch, Swedish, Continental, South African, Australasian; numerous photos of individual athletes and leading athletic teams. Price 10 cents.

No. 27—College Athletics.

M. C. Murphy, the well-known athletic trainer, now with Pennsylvania, the author of this book, has written it especially for the schoolboy and college man, but it is invaluable for the athlete who wishes to excel in any branch of athletic sport; profusely illustrated. Price 10 cents.

No. 182—All-Around Athletics.

Gives in full the method of scoring the All-Around Championship; how to train for the All-Around Championship. Illustrated. Price 10 cents.

No. 156—Athlete's Guide.

Full instructions for the beginner, telling how to sprint, hurdle, jump and throw weights, general hints on training; valuable advice to beginners and important A. A. U. rules and their explanations, while the pictures comprise many scenes of champions in action. Price 10 cents.

SPALDING ATHLETIC LIBRARY

No. 273—The Olympic Games at Athens.

A complete account of the Olympic Games of 1906, at Athens, the greatest International Athletic Contest ever held. Compiled by J. E. Sullivan, Special United States Commissioner to the Olympic Games. Price 10 cents.

No. 87—Athletic Primer.

Edited by J. E. Sullivan, Ex-President of the Amateur Athletic Union. Tells how to organize an athletic club, how to conduct an athletic meeting, and gives rules for the government of athletic meetings; contents also include directions for laying out athletic grounds, and a very instructive article on training. Price 10 cents.

No. 252—How to Sprint.

Every athlete who aspires to be a sprinter can study this book to advantage. Price 10 cents.

No. 255—How to Run 100 Yards.

By J. W. Morton, the noted British champion. Many of Mr. Morton's methods of training are novel to American athletes, but his success is the best tribute to their worth. Illustrated. Price 10 cents.

No. 174—Distance and Cross-Country Running.

By George Orton, the famous University of Pennsylvania runner. The quarter, half, mile, the longer distances, and cross-country running and steeplechasing, with instructions for training; pictures of leading athletes in action, with comments by the editor. Price 10 cents.

No. 259—Weight Throwing.

Probably no other man in the world has had the varied and long experience of James S. Mitchel, the author, in the weight throwing department of athletics. The book gives valuable information not only for the novice, but for the expert as well. Price 10 cents

No. 246—Athletic Training for Schoolboys.

By Geo. W. Orton. Each event in the intercollegiate programme is treated of separately. Price 10 cents.

No. 55—Official Sporting Rules.

Contains rules not found in other publications for the government of many sports; rules for wrestling, shuffleboard, snowshoeing, professional racing, pigeon shooting, dog racing, pistol and revolver shooting, British water polo rules, Rugby football rules. Price 10 cents.

ATHLETIC AUXILIARIES.

No. 311—Official Handbook of the A.A.U.

The A. A. U. is the governing body of athletes in the United States of America, and all games must be held under its rules, which are exclusively published in this handbook, and a copy should be in the hands of every athlete and every club officer in America. Price 10 cents.

No. 316—Official Intercollegiate A.A.A.A. Handbook.

Contains constitution, by-laws, and laws of athletics; records from 1876 to date. Price 10 cents.

No. 308—Official Handbook New York Interscholastic Athletic Association.

Contains the Association's records, constitution and by-laws and other information. Price 10 cents.

No. 302—Official Y.M.C.A. Handbook.

Contains the official rules governing all sports under the jurisdiction of the Y. M. C. A., official Y. M. C. A. scoring tables, pentathlon rules, pictures of leading Y. M. C. A. athletes. Price 10 cents.

No. 313—Official Handbook of the Public Schools Athletic League.

Edited by Dr. C. Ward Crampton, director of physical education in the Public Schools of Greater New York. Illustrated. Price 10 cents.

SPALDING ATHLETIC LIBRARY

No. 314—Official Handbook Girls' Branch of the Public Schools Athletic League.

The official publication. Contains: constitution and by-laws, list of officers, donors, founders, life and annual members, reports and illustrations. Price 10 cents.

No. 331—Schoolyard Athletics.

By J. E. Sullivan, Ex-President Amateur Athletic Union and member of Board of Education of Greater New York. An invaluable handbook for the teacher and the pupil. Gives a systematic plan for conducting school athletic contests and instructs how to prepare for the various events. Illustrated. Price 10 cents.

No. 317—Marathon Running.

A new and up-to-date book on this popular pastime. Contains pictures of the leading Marathon runners, methods of training, and best times made in various Marathon events. Price 10 cents.

Group XIII. Athletic Accomplishments

No. 177—How to Swim.

Will interest the expert as well as the novice; the illustrations were made from photographs especially posed, showing the swimmer in clear water; a valuable feature is the series of "land drill" exercises for the beginner. Price 10 cents.

No. 296—Speed Swimming.

By Champion C. M. Daniels of the New York Athletic Club team, holder of numerous American records, and the best swimmer in America qualified to write on the subject. Any boy should be able to increase his speed in the water after reading Champion Daniels' instructions on the subject. Price 10 cents.

No. 128—How to Row.

By E. J. Giannini, of the New York Athletic Club, one of America's most famous amateur oarsmen and champions. Shows how to hold the oars, the finish of the stroke and other valuable information. Price 10 cents.

No. 23—Canoeing.

Paddling, sailing, cruising and racing canoes and their uses; with hints on rig and management; the choice of a canoe; sailing canoes, racing regulations; canoeing and camping. Fully illustrated. Price 10 cents.

No. 209—How to Become a Skater.

Contains advice for beginners; how to become a figure skater, showing how to do all the different tricks of the best figure skaters. Pictures of prominent skaters and numerous diagrams. Price 10 cents.

No. 282—Official Roller Skating Guide.

Directions for becoming a fancy and trick roller skater, and rules for roller skating. Pictures of prominent trick skaters in action. Price 10 cents.

No. 178—How to Train for Bicycling.

Gives methods of the best riders when training for long or short distance races; hints on training. Revised and up-to-date in every particular. Price 10 cents.

Group XIV. Manly Sports

No. 140—Wrestling.

Catch-as-catch-can style. Seventy illustrations of the different holds, photographed especially and so described that anybody can with little effort learn every one. Price 10 cents.

No. 18—Fencing.

By Dr. Edward Breck, of Boston, editor of The Swordsman, a prominent amateur fencer. A book that has stood the test of time, and is universally acknowledged to be a standard work. Illustrated. Price 10 cents.

SPALDING ATHLETIC LIBRARY

No. 162—Boxing Guide.
Contains over 70 pages of illustrations showing all the latest blows, posed especially for this book under the supervision of a well-known instructor of boxing, who makes a specialty of teaching and knows how to impart his knowledge. Price 10 cents.

No. 165—The Art of Fencing
By Regis and Louis Senac, of New York, famous instructors and leading authorities on the subject. Gives in detail how every move should be made. Price 10 cents.

No. 236—How to Wrestle.
The most complete and up-to-date book on wrestling ever published. Edited by F. R. Toombs, and devoted principally to special poses and illustrations by George Hackenschmidt, the "Russian Lion." Price 10 cents.

No. 102—Ground Tumbling.
Any boy, by reading this book and following the instructions, can become proficient. Price 10 cents.

No. 289—Tumbling for Amateurs.
Specially compiled for amateurs by Dr. James T. Gwathmey. Every variety of the pastime explained by text and pictures, over 100 different positions being shown. Price 10 cents.

No. 191—How to Punch the Bag.
The best treatise on bag punching that has ever been printed. Every variety of blow used in training is shown and explained, with a chapter on fancy bag punching by a well-known theatrical bag puncher. Price 10 cents.

No. 200—Dumb-Bells.
The best work on dumb-bells that has ever been offered. By Prof. G. Bojus, of New York. Contains 200 photographs. Should be in the hands of every teacher and pupil of physical culture, and is invaluable for home exercise. Price 10 cents.

No. 143—Indian Clubs and Dumb-Bells.
By America's amateur champion club swinger, J. H. Dougherty. It is clearly illustrated, by which any novice can become an expert. Price 10 cents.

No. 262—Medicine Ball Exercises.
A series of plain and practical exercises with the medicine ball, suitable for boys and girls, business and professional men, in and out of gymnasium. Price 10 cents.

No. 29—Pulley Weight Exercises.
By Dr. Henry S. Anderson, instructor in heavy gymnastics Yale gymnasium. In conjunction with a chest machine anyone with this book can become perfectly developed. Price 10 cents.

No. 233—Jiu Jitsu.
Each move thoroughly explained and illustrated with numerous full-page pictures of Messrs. A. Minami and K. Koyama, two of the most famous exponents of the art of Jiu Jitsu, who posed especially for this book. Price 10 cents.

No. 166—How to Swing Indian Clubs.
By Prof. E. B. Warman. By following the directions carefully anyone can become an expert. Price 10 cents.

No. 326—Professional Wrestling.
A book devoted to the catch-as-catch-can style; illustrated with half-tone pictures showing the different holds used by Frank Gotch, champion catch-as-catch-can wrestler of the world. Posed by Dr. Roller and Charles Postl. By Ed. W. Smith, Sporting Editor of the Chicago American. Price 10 cents.

Group XV. Gymnastics

No. 104—The Grading of Gymnastic Exercises.
By G. M. Martin. A book that should be in the hands of every physical director of the Y. M. C. A., school, club, college, etc. Price 10 cents.

SPALDING ATHLETIC LIBRARY

No. 214—Graded Calisthenics and Dumb-Bell Drills.
For years it has been the custom in most gymnasiums of memorizing a set drill, which was never varied. Consequently the beginner was given the same kind and amount as the older member. With a view to giving uniformity the present treatise is attempted. Price 10 cents.

No. 254—Barnjum Bar Bell Drill.
Edited by Dr. R. Tait McKenzie, Director Physical Training, University of Pennsylvania. Profusely illustrated. Price 10 cents.

No. 158—Indoor and Outdoor Gymnastic Games.
A book that will prove valuable to indoor and outdoor gymnasiums, schools, outings and gatherings where there are a number to be amused. Price 10 cents.

No. 124—How to Become a Gymnast.
By Robert Stoll, of the New York A. C., the American champion on the flying rings from 1885 to 1892. Any boy can easily become proficient with a little practice. Price 10 cents.

No. 287—Fancy Dumb Bell and Marching Drills.
All concede that games and recreative exercises during the adolescent period are preferable to set drills and monotonous movements. These drills, while designed primarily for boys, can be used successfully with girls and men and women. Profusely illustrated. Price 10 cents.

No. 327—Pyramid Building Without Apparatus.
By W. J. Cromie, Instructor of Gymnastics, University of Pennsylvania. With illustrations showing many different combinations. This book should be in the hands of all gymnasium instructors. Price 10 Cents.

No. 328—Exercises on the Parallel Bars.
By W. J. Cromie. Every gymnast should procure a copy of this book. Illustrated with cuts showing many novel exercises. Price 10 cents.

No. 329—Pyramid Building with Chairs, Wands and Ladders.
By W. J. Cromie. Illustrated with half-tone photographs showing many interesting combinations. Price 10 cents.

GYMNASTIC AUXILIARY.

No. 333—Official Handbook Inter-Collegiate Association Amateur Gymnasts of America.
Edited by P. R. Carpenter, Physical Director Amherst College. Contains pictures of leading teams and individual champions, official rules governing contests, records. Price 10 cents.

Group XVI. Physical Culture

No. 161—Ten Minutes' Exercise for Busy Men.
By Dr. Luther Halsey Gulick, Director of Physical Training in the New York Public Schools. A concise and complete course of physical education. Price 10 cents.

No. 208—Physical Education and Hygiene.
This is the fifth of the Physical Training series, by Prof. E. B. Warman (see Nos. 142, 149, 166, 185, 213, 261, 290.) Price 10 cents.

No. 149—The Care of the Body.
A book that all who value health should read and follow its instructions. By Prof. E. B. Warman, the well-known lecturer and authority on physical culture. Price 10 cents.

No. 142—Physical Training Simplified.
By Prof. E. B. Warman. A complete, thorough and practical book where the whole man is considered—brain and body. Price 10 cents.

SPALDING ATHLETIC LIBRARY

No. 185—Health Hints.
By Prof. E. B. Warman. Health influenced by insulation; health influenced by underwear; health influenced by color; exercise. Price 10 cents.

No. 213—285 Health Answers.
By Prof. E. B. Warman. Contents: ventilating a bedroom; ventilating a house; how to obtain pure air; bathing; salt water baths at home; a substitute for ice water; to cure insomnia, etc., etc. Price 10 cents.

No. 238—Muscle Building.
By Dr. L. H. Gulick. A complete treatise on the correct method of acquiring strength. Illustrated. Price 10 cents.

No. 234—School Tactics and Maze Running.
A series of drills for the use of schools. Edited by Dr. Luther Halsey Gulick. Price 10 cents.

No. 261—Tensing Exercises.
By Prof. E. B. Warman. The "Tensing" or "Resisting" system of muscular exercises is the most thorough, the most complete, the most satisfactory, and the most fascinating of systems. Price 10 cents.

No. 285—Health; by Muscular Gymnastics.
With hints on right living. By W. J. Cromie. If one will practice the exercises and observe the hints therein contained, he will be amply repaid for so doing. Price 10 cents.

No. 288—Indigestion Treated by Gymnastics
By W. J. Cromie. If the hints therein contained are observed and the exercises faithfully performed great relief will be experienced. Price 10 cents.

No. 290—Get Well; Keep Well.
By Prof. E. B. Warman, author of a number of books in the Spalding Athletic Library on physical training. Price 10 cents.

No. 325—Twenty Minute Exercises.
By Prof. E. B. Warman, with chapters on "How to Avoid Growing Old," and "Fasting; Its Objects and Benefits." Price 10 cents.

No. 330—Physical Training for the School and Class Room.
Edited by G. R. Borden, Physical Director of the Y. M. C. A., Easton, Pa. A book that is for practical work in the school room. Illustrated. Price 10 cents.

L. DeB. HANDLEY.

CONTENTS

	PAGE
Introduction	5
Evolution of the American Game	9
How the Game is Played To-day in America	13
Preparatory Work	17
How to Develop the Green Player	21
Choosing the Players	26
Developing the Team	31
On Fouling	32
Preparing for a Contest	34
A Few Points for the Game	35
American Rules of Water Polo	37

1—Otto Wahle, N.Y.A.C., and J. A. Jarvis, England, at Leicester, Eng.
2—A. M. Goersling, Missouri A.C., Breast Stroke, Champion and Record Holder. 3—E. H. Adams, New York A.C., Plunging Champion and Record Holder, 1903. 4—C. A. Ruberl, N.Y.A.C. National Back Stroke Champion. New York A.C. Relay Team. (National A.A.U. Champions.)
5—C. M. Daniels, 6—T. E. Kitching, Jr. 7—C. D. Trubenbach. 8—L. S. Crane.

INTRODUCTION

The value of an athletic game or contest is determined by four things: Its physical culture merits; its utility; its attractiveness as a pastime, and its spectacular features.

Water polo has few equals as a means of developing the body. The swimming alone in it would insure general and symmetrical development, but the player wrestles besides, during a game, and every part of the body is given its proportionate share of this gruelling work, developing all muscles in a uniform way.

As to its utility, it is self-evident. Swimming has come to be looked upon as a necessity, simply because it may be the means of saving life, and in this water polo is the most practical of teachers. A player is coached on how to free himself from every kind of a tackle, how to assist an exhausted team mate and how to apply the best methods of resuscitation when anyone is knocked out. Then these teachings have to be practised frequently while the team is at work and one becomes proficient insensibly and as a matter of course. It is a revelation to see an expert player handle a drowning person, and more especially a frantic one. The rescue is performed in such an easy, matter-of-fact way as to lead one to wonder at the halo of heroism that surrounds most cases of life saving. Hardly a player but has several rescues to his credit, which he looks upon as a series of trifling services rendered to fellow mortal, and no more.

As a pastime water polo is among the leaders. Hard and exhausting it may be, but there is an exhilaration in dashing about the pool, fighting one's way to goal, that no other game gives. And it has a feature that appeals strongly to the man who has attained manhood and its numerous responsibilities: the rarity of accidents. Bruises and knockouts one gets a-plenty, but those serious injuries which marr foot ball, hockey and lacrosse are totally unknown.

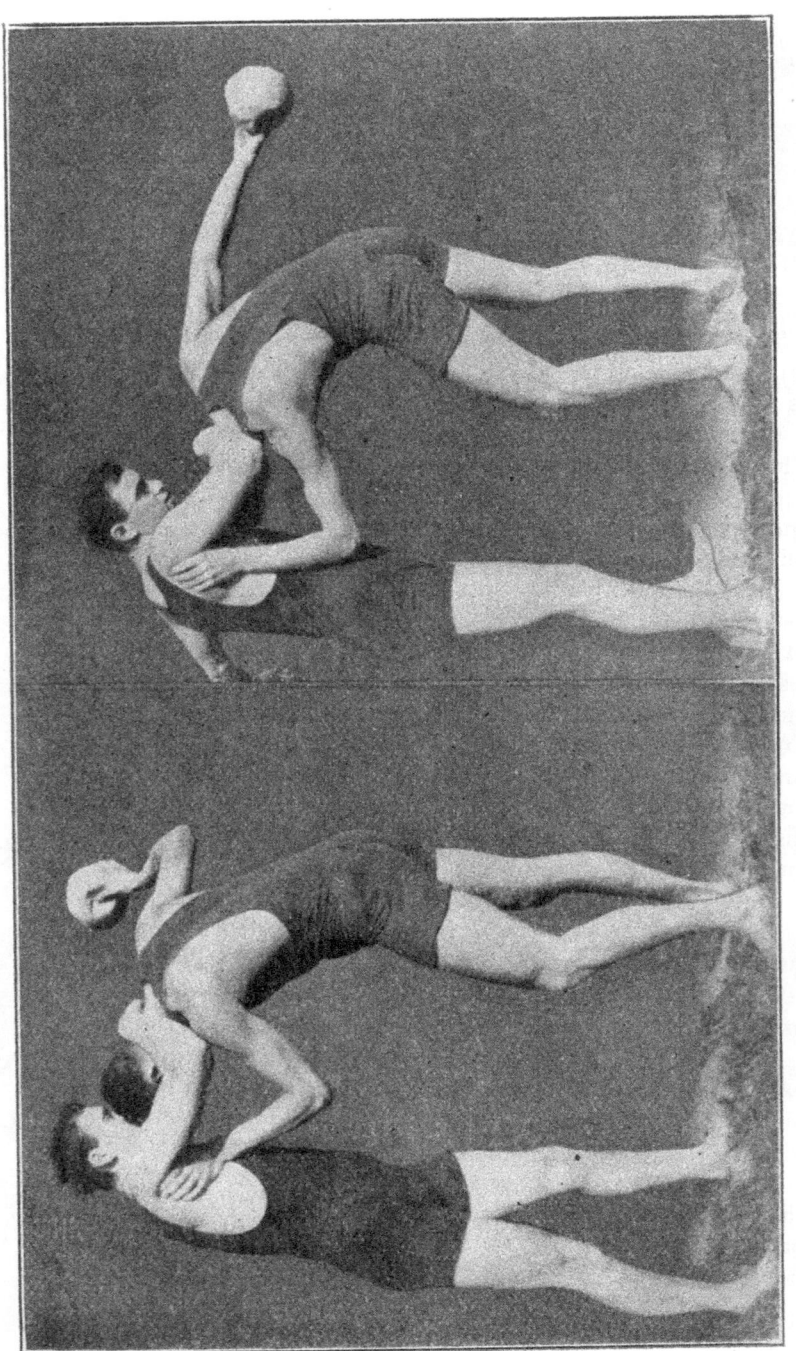

Fig. A. Dodging. Fig. B. Passing under and turning on back.
HOW A TACKLE IS ELUDED.

Lastly. From the spectator's standpoint, the game is fascinating. To most people the mere disporting of a dozen expert swimmers is an exhibition well worth seeing, and when to this is added the zest of a clever and keen contest, replete with brilliant action and exciting encounter, no more attractive show can be imagined.

FIG. C. HOW A TACKLE IS ELUDED—Over and free.

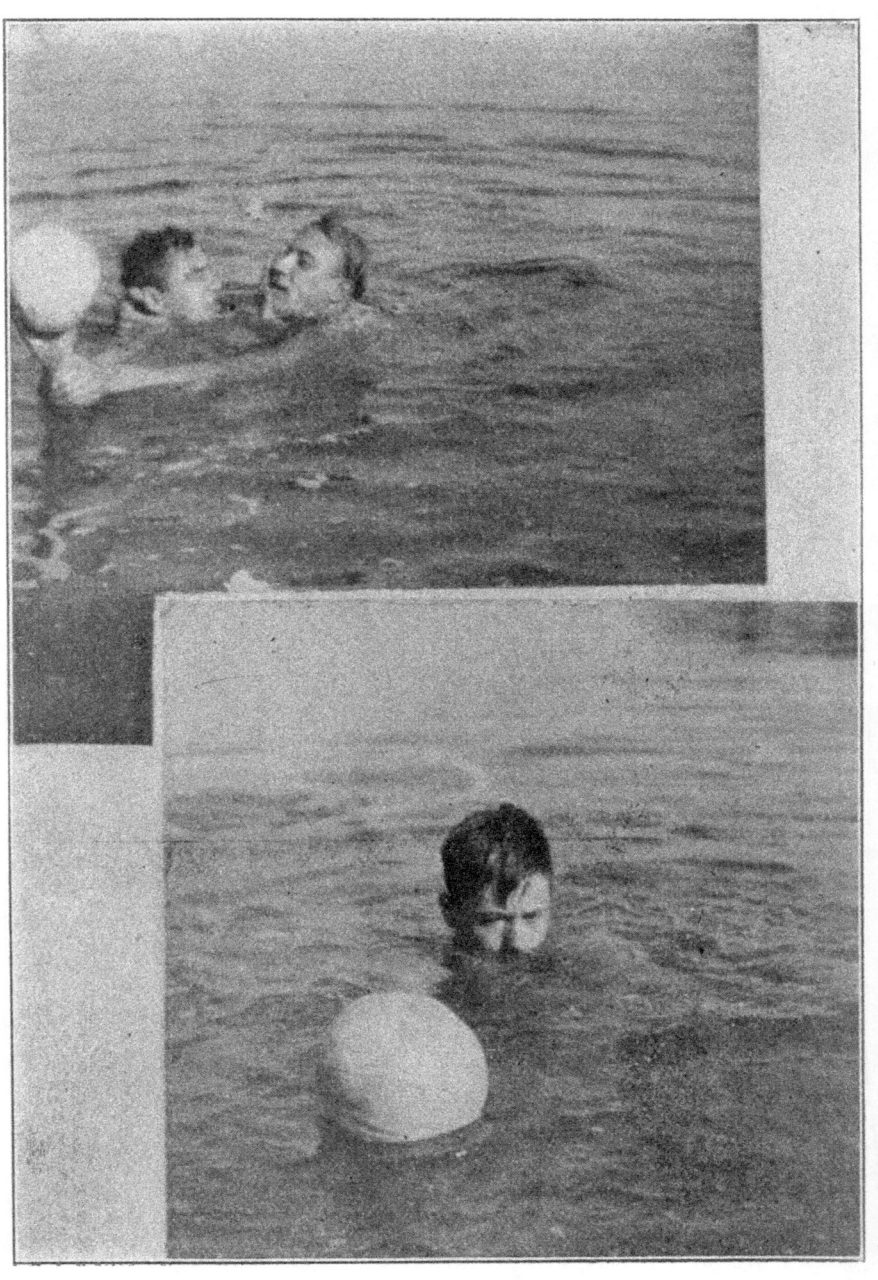

Fig. D. ONE WAY OF GETTING THE BALL.
Fig. E. FLIPPING BACK THE BALL.

EVOLUTION OF THE AMERICAN GAME

There is a belief that a game similar to water polo was played by the ancients, but no actual proof of it has been found. Rules were first formulated in England in 1870, and we adopted them in America about 1890, but our present game bears absolutely no resemblance to the one that was then played. In the latter, points were scored by throwing an inflated rubber ball nine inches in diameter through an open goal marked by uprights and a cross bar; and passing was the feature of the game. Americans found it unsuited. The few available tanks were so small that there was no space for action, and the outdoor season was too short to be satisfactory.

The idea was then conceived of changing the goal into a solid surface, four feet by one in size, and to oblige the scorer to touch the ball to the goal while holding it, instead of passing it.

The innovation met ready favor, but, as may be imagined, transformed the game. From an open passing one water polo became one of close formations and fierce scrimmages. These, at first, were disorderly scuffles, where weight and brute strength reigned supreme, but little by little strict rules were formulated to eliminate rough tactics and then science became an important factor.

In 1897 a man entered the field who was destined to revolutionize the system of play.

Harold H. Reeder, of the late Knickerbocker Athletic A. C., besides being a good leader and a brilliant individual player, knew how to handle men. He realized that in a growing sport new ideas would mean development, and he made it possible for the members of his squad to experiment with those they had. The system he used is worth a few words of explanation, be-

Fig. G. SCORING ON A HURDLE OVER A TEAM-MATE.
Fig. H. ONE WAY OF BREAKING A TACKLE.

cause it was accountable for the wonderful strides made since 1897, and because every team will profit by its adoption.

Reeder, well aided by Prof. Alex Meffett, began by teaching every candidate the rudiments of the game; veterans and greenhorns alike were put through the mill. Each was schooled in the principles of swimming, diving, catching, passing, scoring, interfering, tackling and breaking, until these points had been thoroughly mastered, and only then did the team practise begin. But again, no player was allowed in unprepared. Reeder instituted blackboard practice and saw that everyone attended it. Placing before his assembled squad the possible formations, he made players selected at random explain the duties of every position in each formation. By this system he obliged every player to use his brains, and he found out the amount of water polo intelligence that each possessed. He also imparted to each the ideas of all the others, he taught them how to fill every position and he brought to light many new plays.

The progress which the innovation was responsible for no one realized until the aggregation of yearlings from the Knickerbocker Athletic Club defeated the formidable array of champions representing the New York Athletic Club. Reeder abandoned the game two years later, but his good work lived after him and some of his team mates held the championship for many years by following his teachings.

Fig. J. HOW TO GET A SAFE GRIP ON THE BALL.
Fingers are sunk into the rubber.

Fig. I HOW TO TAKE THE BALL FROM A FORWARD AFTER TACKLING HIM.

HOW THE GAME IS PLAYED TO-DAY IN AMERICA

Water polo as played to-day in America is rather dangerous for outdoors, and indoor pools are generally used. It is a contest between two teams of six, having as object the touching of the opponent's goalboard with an inflated rubber ball seven inches in diameter, which the referee throws into the water at start of play.

In order to score, the ball has to be touched to the goal while in the hand of a player; it cannot be thrown. The goals are spaces four by one foot, situated at each short end of the playing area, eighteen inches above the water level. The size of the playing area is optional, though the recognized dimensions are 60 x 40 feet or 25 x 75 feet, with a uniform depth of seven feet of water. Imaginary lines are drawn across the tank (see Fig. T), parallel to the short ends, at four and fifteen feet from them. The first, called four-foot line, serves as protection to the goal tenders and cannot be crossed until the ball is within; the other is the foul line and serves to mark the spot on which the forwards line up on being given a free trial. The four-foot line also marks the goal section, a space 4 x 8 feet, in which indiscriminate tackling is allowed when the ball is within. .

Each team of six is divided into a forward line (centre, right forward and left forward) whose duty it is to attack the opponent's goal; and a backfield of three (half-back, right goaltender and left goal-tender) upon whom devolves the defense of the home goal.

At the start of play the two teams line up at their respective ends (see Fig. Q), the referee places the ball in the middle of the playing area and then blows a whistle. At this signal the twelve players dive in, the forwards to make a dash for the

Fig. K. HOW THE FORWARD PROTECTS HIS TEAMMATE—Method used in breaking the hold of a back who is tackling the man with the ball.

Fig. L. A HIGH TACKLE—Encircling the forward with arms over the right shoulder and under the left, by which method the tackle keeps his head above water while submerging antagonist.

ball, the backs to take up their positions. The forward who first reaches the ball tosses it back to the defense men (see Fig. E) who hold it until the line of attack is formed and then pass it back. Immediately a fierce scrimmage takes place and either a score is made or the ball changes side and a scrimmage occurs at the other end. After a score the teams line up as at start of play.

Time of play is sixteen minutes, actual, divided into two halves of eight minutes each, with an intermission of five minutes between halves. Only two substitutes are allowed, and they can only be used to replace an injured or exhausted player.

FIG. F. SCORING OVER AN OPPONENT BY TACKLING HIM HIGH.

FIG. M. A GOOD TACKLE—Showing also how the forward holds the ball out of reach of his assailant.
FIG. N. A HOPELESS NECK HOLD—Showing one method of taking the ball away from the forward.

PREPARATORY WORK

No man should attempt to play water polo who is not in the best possible physical condition. Before joining the squad, every candidate, be he a novice coming to learn the game, or a veteran resuming training, should prepare himself for the hard work in sight. I don't mean that he should be down to edge, but in good ruddy health. As a matter of fact, a man is far better off if he can start the season with eight or ten pounds of extra avoirdupois; and four or five pounds above "pink of condition" may be carried throughout the season with good result. They will prevent one's getting cold while in the water and keep one from going stale, a very easy matter in water polo.

Preliminary exercise should be taken daily for a week or two in anticipation of starting practise. Long swims are advisable at this early date, but should be abandoned while preparing for a contest as one sprints only in a game.

The best system to follow is a very simple one.

A few minutes in the steam room (not more than five) or some calisthenics to warm up the blood, then a fast hundred. This done, rest until you have regained your breath. Taking the water polo ball next, pass it to given points of the tank to secure accuracy and sprint after it each time. Then get against the side of the tank and placing the ball ten or twelve feet away, try to secure it with one hand on a push-off. This, done half a dozen times daily, will ensure accurate passing, catching and obviate fumbling.

Another excellent exercise is to place the ball fifteen or twenty feet from you and then swim after it under water, trying to get it without coming to the surface. This has the double object of getting you used to underwater work and accustoms you to looking for the ball while submerged in a scrimmage.

FIG. O. When the man with the ball faces you and has his right arm out in front to protect himself against your tackle, seize his right wrist with your right hand and twist him around fast until—
(FIG. P.) his back is towards you and you can put a back hold on him; then he is at your mercy, and you can take the ball from him.

Gymnasium work is not advisable unless one's physical condition is badly in need of building up, and even then only the lightest kind should be taken. It has too great a tendency to harden the muscles; a swimmer's should be soft and pliable.

Breathing exercise can be highly recommended, there is nothing better for the wind. A good system is to take it while walking in the open air. By inhaling for the space of six steps, and exhaling for six, the lungs are properly worked. In cold weather breathe through the nose.

In regard to food, a hearty mixed diet is the best. One may also take a little beer, ale or claret, at dinner, with beneficial effect.

Smoking, on the other hand, is harmful, and one should abstain from tobacco in any form. As for tea, coffee, drugs and intoxicants, they should be used in great moderation.

A habit which is prevalent and which is the cause of many ills is the standing around the pool, wet. This should be avoided. If you want to watch what is going on, dry off thoroughly, and put on a bathrobe.

In going into the water, never forget to place cotton in your ears, and again when you come out change it for a fresh piece, until the ear is dry. Cold in the ear and other complaints can thus be avoided.

Do not abuse the steam and hot rooms, they are the death of snap.

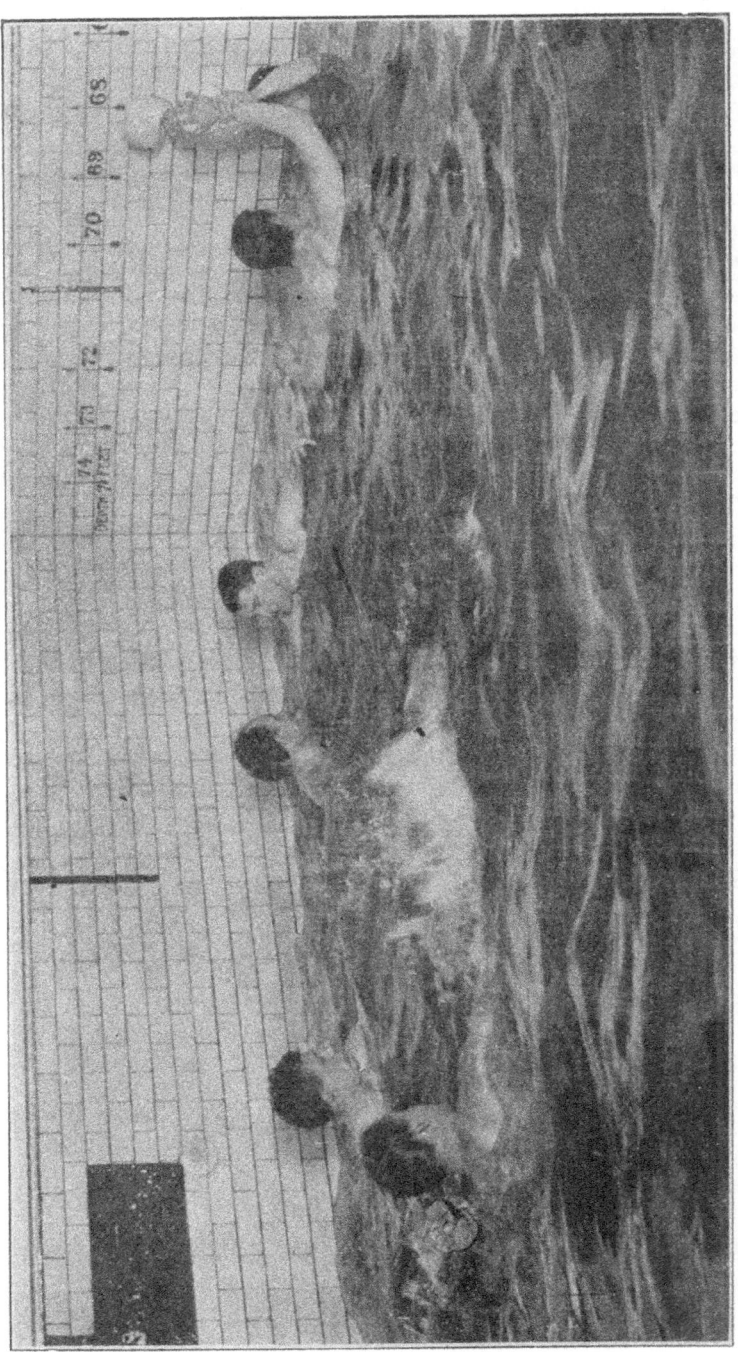

A FOUL.—ATTACKING FORWARD HAS CROSSED FOUR-FOOT LINE AHEAD OF THE BALL.

HOW TO DEVELOP THE GREEN PLAYER

The game of water polo is such a strenuous one that even the best of men often tackle it with misgivings. The green player should on no account attempt to take part even in a scrub game until he has thoroughly mastered the rudiments. The man who goes in against an experienced tackler, ignorant of the means of protecting himself, receives punishment so severe as to give him a completely erroneous idea of the game.

If the candidate has followed the suggestions given above he will be physically able to stand the gruelling, but more is needed; he should be able to take care of himself. To teach him how, he must be taken in hand alone, and shown the various tackles and breaks.

This is best done on terra firma; in the water the man will be thinking of the ducking in sight and his mind will not be in receptive mood. It is also essential to make him understand a hold thoroughly before proceeding with another.

Once a man has the movements learned, he can be put in the water with a skilled player and allowed to practise on the latter, who should let him secure the holds without opposition at first, but gradually increase the resistance until he becomes proficient. If there is no one to coach and no good player to practise against the new men should work on each other.

Water polo holds are a good deal a matter of individuality, each man builds up a set of his own, but one tackle and one break will serve as a foundation for all.

To learn the tackle, give your co-worker the ball and let him come toward you. When he's a couple of feet off, take a good hard stroke, lift yourself as high out of the water as you can, throw your arm around his neck, and pulling his head down until

A GOOD SCORE ON A HURDLE PLAY.

it is jammed hard against your chest, wind your legs around his body (see Fig. M). Then you have him at your mercy, and you can proceed to take the ball away from him. This tackle should be learned by forwards and backs alike, all need it.

The best break known (see Figs. A, B, C) is the following: We will suppose that you carry the ball in the right hand. On approaching your opponent throw your left shoulder forward, presenting a three-quarter view. To tackle you effectively he must use his right arm, as you could easily repel a left-handed one in your position. As soon as his right arm goes up, place your left hand squarely under his armpit (Fig. A) and let yourself sink, twisting around (Fig. B), face toward him, as you pass under, and as soon as you are on your back force his body over you. Then plant both feet on him (Fig. C) and shove off. In most cases, if you succeed, you will find yourself between your opponent and his goal, where all you have to do is to touch the board for a score.

To use the legs at every possible chance should be a principle of the player. Once an opponent is caught in a good leg-hold he is rendered helpless. Incidentally, the wise player ceases struggling when he recognizes that he is caught beyond freeing. It is an excellent rule also to avoid being tackled uselessly; if a body encounter is liable to let you out best, or will help your side, go into it heart and soul, just as hard as you know how, but never make a senseless sacrifice.

Passing and catching are all important factors in water polo and should be practised constantly. In passing it is well to bear in mind that the object in view is to give the ball securely to one's team mate. Pass high and carefully; a low throw may be intercepted and a hard one fumbled. Specially in close quarters high passing is essential.

To cover one's opponent when the other side has the ball and get away from him when one's own has it, should be the religion of every player. In covering him, always stay back of him, where you can watch him, and tackle him just in the nick of time if the ball is passed to him.

THE START OF A GAME—PLAYERS LINED UP, AWAITING THE REFEREE'S WHISTLE.

Many green men have an idea that one knows intuitively how to score, but it is not so. The various ways must be learned. One only does in a game what one has become used to in practise, for there is little time or chance to think in the excitement of a keen contest, and it is those things which have been ground into one by dint of repetition that stand by one. To get used to scoring place yourself three or four yards from goal and then sink yourself, or let someone else put you under, and try to come up and hit the board with eyes closed; you will soon find what a difference practise makes. You must also learn how to hurdle by letting someone tread water between you and goal and score by placing your free hand on his shoulder and lifting yourself over.

A short course of the above and you will be ready to line up.

CHOOSING THE PLAYERS

In choosing players to form a team the fact should be taken into consideration that there are many attributes which go to making the good player. Speed in swimming, tackling ability, strength, endurance, pluck, aggressiveness, alertness in taking advantage of opportunities, good handling of the ball, good watermanship, underwater skill, coolness in trying moments, good head and willingness to sacrifice brilliant individual achievements to team work should all count in the decision. The strongest, hardest and best tackler in the world will be of no use whatsoever if he has no head. A weak tackler who knows how to husband his resources and bring them into play at the right moment is worth twice as much.

For centre a big man and a fast one does best; his duty it is to swim for the ball and to protect the scorer. For forwards take men who are good at underwater work, who are aggressive and plucky, who are broad-minded enough not to care who scores as long as the team gets the point, who will know how to seize opportunities in a flash and who knows not what it is to give in.

For half-back an endurant swimmer is needed who can stand plenty of work and who can be taught to cover his man without letting him get out of reach under any pretext. And as goal-tenders put cool-headed men, preferably heavy ones, who can tackle hard and know how to hold their tackles. Never allow a nervous or excitable player on the defense.

The team chosen, it should be lined up for practise, but before we go into the team work let us look over the duties of the different positions.

THE FORWARDS.

Upon the three forwards rests the task of scoring points for their team. They have by now learned all that they need know individually, and they must be taught how to attack the enemy's camp together.

The aim of the forwards should be to eliminate either by force or by stratagem one of the backs. In olden days this was accomplished by rushing four men instead of three, at start of play, then if the attack failed it meant a score to the other side. Modern water polo teaches how three can score against three. A good way to eliminate the half-back is to mass around him. When he is surrounded the man he turns his back to tackles him from behind and shoves him under hard; then, before he can come to the surface again all three spring at the two remaining defenders. The speed at which this play is executed generally accounts for its success or failure. It is the quick opening of the foot ball game.

At start of play the centre swims for the ball and the other two without paying any attention to him go and station themselves just beyond the opponent's four-foot line, one on each side of the tank. If the adversaries get the ball, the centre may fall back to assist the defense, but if he gets it, he passes (he should really flip if he knows how) back to his own goal tenders. Then he proceeds to form his line of attack, the ball is passed back to him (he is generally the free man, as both forwards are covered), and he dashes into the goal tender giving the ball at the same time to the man who is to carry it in.

It may be well here to caution the forwards against crossing the four-foot line ahead of the ball; it is a foul and kills a score. They should also watch the back who is covering them closely. If one attempts to swim down and help the attack he should be followed so as to equalize matters.

The forwards must never attack shoulder to shoulder, as it enables one back to take two men and leaves the other back free.

Coming now to the system of attack, there are three formations around which all others are built. By learning them well a team will know quite as much water polo as is necessary to win. The trouble with most teams is that they pay too much attention to tricks and too little to straight polo.

The first formation is for an underwater goal. The forwards advance on a line. The man carrying the ball precedes the others into the four-foot line and allows himself to be jumped, meeting the goal tender with the break shown in Figs. A, B, C; if he succeeds in evading the tackle and getting through, he just touches the board for a point. Meanwhile as the goal tender jumps him, the centre tackles the goal tender and puts on him the tackle shown in Fig. K, which often frees the under man and allows him to score. Quick movements both on the part of the scorer and of the centre, as well as speed in approaching, better one's chances a lot. In this play the other forward just covers the third back and keeps in readiness to secure the ball if it is fumbled.

The second formation is for the hurdle. We will suppose the right forward is to score. The ball is given to the left forward, and centre gets outside of the left goal tender. Then the ball is passed to right forward who promptly passes into the goal section; immediately, centre tackles left goal tender and before the right goal tender can circle them, right forward leans on centre's shoulder, lifts himself over, and scores as in Fig. G. This play is not practicable when the defense plays two half-backs and only one goal tender, unless one of the half-backs is drawn over. But occasions often present themselves in a game where the hurdle can be used.

The last formation which has come to be practised a lot of late consists in having the forwards tackle the three defense men individually, pass the ball into the goal section and trust to getting there first. It's a good play, but an awfully risky one, and I think if records had been kept they would show many more failures than successes.

The hundreds of other formations incidental to these three cannot be gone into, but even one of these plays mastered to perfection will win every game. For the unexpected results of failures to score directly on these formations, no system can be advocated; they make opportunities for the quick-witted.

It is well to repeat here that while the forwards are trying these formations the backs should only tackle lightly so as to get them used to the work necessary, after breaking through. As times goes by, though, the tackles should gradually be made harder.

All players should remember, too, that the preliminary exercises advocated earlier in this book will be very beneficial if kept up throughout the period of active training.

THE BACKS.

There are two systems of defense now in vogue. In one, two goal-tenders, stationed on either side of the goal and one half-back patroling the fifteen-foot line, are used. In the other one goal-tender guards the goal and two half-backs cover the opponent forwards. The former system is distinctive of the East, the latter of the West.

Much can be said in favor of each. With a fast set of backs the Western method is more efficient, with a slow one it is often fatal. A great point made by advocates of the two half-back system is that it kills the forwards' chances of team work since each man is practically covered by his adversary. This may and may not be an advantage. If a forward stronger than his opposing back is found, a score cannot be avoided in this coupling system every time the said forward gets the ball. All that can be said to the backs about this disposition of players is: Cover your men like shadows; never let them get out of reach of your hand, and perfect yourself in the art of taking the ball away from an opponent so that you can come out best in every dual encounter. It is simplified playing.

For the Eastern game the two goal-tenders should station themselves about a foot to each side of the goal and the half-back hover around the opposing centre, and never let him out of his sight, tackling him without mercy every time the ball is within four feet. In this he should be particularly careful on the underwater play; the centre should never be allowed to get a hold on the back who is tackling the man with the ball.

The hurdle will be impossible if the half-back sticks to the centre and the throw-in can be avoided by the backs tackling high so that they have their head above water while the others are submerged, thus having the best chance to reach the ball first and pass it out.

A good tackle for the goal-tenders is in Fig. L. Forward has ball in right hand held up behind him; jump high and land in front of him with body upright, legs open and arms wide; throw right arm over his left shoulder, left arm under his right armpit, and close legs about his waist. Now put your chin on his head and hold him under until the ball comes up.

Goal-tenders should not play too close together and should on no account let go of a tackle until the ball is above water. The half-back should stick to one man and not try to play the entire forward trio. It will tire him out to no purpose. All three should be on the alert for low passes. An intercepted ball by taking the possibility of an attack from the forwards may mean a score to you and maybe the winning point. If unable to secure it, bat it out, take a quick push-off and get there first.

DEVELOPING THE TEAM

After the players have been chosen and given their positions which they seem best fitted for, it is wise to keep them there and not shift them about daily as some coaches do. Blackboard practice is commendable, specially with a green team, for it gives each man a clear idea of his own duties as well as of those of all his team mates.

To develop the team only the six players should be used. The three forwards line up on the fifteen-foot line and the three backs behind the four-foot line. Let a sort of signal practice be indulged in first, allowing the forwards to go through the process of scoring without opposition, then, as I've indicated before, begin easy tackling and increase by degrees.

Begin with only five or six minutes of work and lengthen a minute at a time every day, until you have the men able to stand twenty minutes of steady work. After practise let them rest for five or ten minutes and then sprint 50 or 100 yards. Practise should not be held every day. Three times a week, with a few sprints on odd days will be quite sufficient.

No man should be allowed to continue when exhausted; it is injurious to him and it may lose a good player to the team, as many who enjoy strenuous games do not care to be punished too severely.

Every man should play as hard as he can in practise; it is the only way of getting used to doing it in a game.

ON FOULING

Strict adherence to rules is one of the things that everyone should be careful of in water polo. It never pays to foul and it often destroys the chances obtained through meritorious work. The rules give the list of punishable offenses, but a few extra recommendations will do no harm. Go into a match prepared to take slugging without retaliation; the man who slugs is not paying attention to his game, and you will eventually get the best of him, while of he offends badly enough to interfere with your playing he will surely be penalized. Crossing the four-foot line is one of the offenses that the forwards commit principally. Tackling by the suit and before the ball is within four feet is the chief fault with the backs.

Three points which need explaining are: Kicking, swimming under water and hanging on to the side of the tank.

Deliberate kicking is absolutely forbidden, but as the man with the ball is allowed to swim on his back, if anyone tries to tackle him while he does so he need not stop his leg movement. On the other hand, if he deliberately kicks to hurt, and the referee can easily see if he does, he will be punished.

Swimming under water with the ball is also forbidden, but it being recognized that a man is often put under by an opponent and could never score unless he retained possession of the ball, allowances have been made. When tackled, a man may cover submerged a distance of not more than eight feet, and no rule forbids his crossing the four-foot line under water. Should one sink purposely though, or be forced under by a team mate, an ensuing score is not allowed and the foul is punished by a free trial to the other side.

Hanging on to the side of the tank for the purpose of resting is permissible. It is only a foul when the player who is hanging on tries to take part in a play. One may be within a yard of where a goal is scored and hang on. Provided no attempt is made to help or prevent a score it is not a foul.

Slugging is a foul at all times and so is unnecessary rough work. For one player to hold the ball over an opponent while another drowns him, simply to put him out of the game, comes under this heading. It is a most unsportsmanly procedure and any fair referee will condemn it and give it the extreme penalty.

PREPARING FOR A CONTEST

A couple of weeks before an important match it is advisable to find scrub teams to practise against the regulars. Split up the forwards and backs by putting them on opposite teams, so that they will play against each other, but let them have the feeling of a real game.

During this period the centre should practise flipping the ball by timing his strokes so as to reach it with arm outstretched (as in Fig. E). It means a lot to have first possession of it, and it is generally secured by a touch only.

Light work should mark the last three or four days, and no steam or hot room. Swim for exercise, and nothing else.

Food has been spoken about, but for at least a week previous to the event pastry, pork, indigestible salads, coffee, tea and intoxicants should be abandoned altogether. Gassy drinks, like soda or ginger ale, are also best left alone. Eat sparingly before practise, and if possible swim on an empty stomach. If you feel at all listless and out of sorts take a day's rest.

On the day of the match try not to change any of your usual habits. It seems a universal habit among athletes to change their food, their drink, their work, and everything else because they are going to compete. It is the very worst thing they can do. Man is too much a creature of habit not to suffer by sudden changes. Keep your mind occupied, too, and away from the worrying thought of what the outcome will be.

A FEW POINTS FOR THE GAME

On entering the tank for an important game every player should forget his individuality and submit passively to the orders of the captain. There must be only one head for a team to succeed, and an order should be executed without hesitation and without questioning; right or wrong, the best results come through blind obedience. The man giving the orders often sees an opening that the other does not.

Let no personal difference affect your game; play to win, not to pay off an old score. It is the goals made, not the men disabled, that give one victory, and victory is what every player should seek.

To the forward, discrimination is a valuable asset. When caught in a tackle so far away from goal that getting free will not help you pass the ball at once, don't allow your opponent to punish you. But if you are nailed within easy reach of goal, fight as long as there is breath of life in you. Never mind how helpless the task may seem, a team mate may come to the rescue at any moment, and then you'll score.

The forward should always play the ball in preference to the man and keep free as much as possible. And above all—play fast and hard.

	GOAL	
	GOAL SECTION	
	4 Ft. Line	
	15 Ft. Line	
	Centre Line	
	15 Ft. Line	
	4 Ft. Line	
	GOAL SECTION	
	GOAL	

AMERICAN RULES OF WATER POLO

I. The ball shall be the regulation white rubber association foot ball not less than 7 inches nor more than 8 inches in diameter.

II. The goals shall be spaces 4 feet long and 12 inches wide marked "Goal" in large letters. One shall be placed at either end of the tank, 18 inches above the water-line equally distant from either side.

III. To score a goal the goal must be touched by the ball in the hand of an opposing player and the greatest number of goals shall count game.

IV. The ball shall be kept on or as near the surface of the water as possible and shall never intentionally be carried under water. No goal shall be allowed when scored by an under-water pass.

V. The contesting teams shall consist of six a side, with two reserve men who can be substituted at any time when the ball is not in play. A player withdrawn cannot return to play. Only six prizes shall be given to the winning team.

VI. Time of play shall be 16 minutes actual time, divided in two halves of 8 minutes each and 5 minutes' rest between halves. Time occupied by disputes, free trials for goal, repairing suits, and lining up after a goal has been scored shall not be reckoned as time of play.

VII. The captains shall be playing members of teams they represent and shall toss for choice of ends of tank. The ends shall be changed at half time.

VIII. The referee shall throw the ball in the centre of the tank and the start for the ball shall be made only at the sound of the whistle.

IX. A ball going out of the tank shall be returned to the place from which it was thrown and given to the opposing team.

X. A mark shall be made four feet from each goal on the side of the tank and an imaginary line between these marks shall be called the four-foot line. No man will be allowed within this line until the ball is within it. The goal tenders, limited to two, of the defending side are alone exempt from this rule. When the ball is within the goal line the goal tenders shall not be allowed any artificial support other than the bottom of the tank.

XI. No player is allowed to interfere with an opponent unless such an opponent is within four feet of the ball, except when the ball is within the goal section, when indiscriminate tackling will be allowed in the goal section. The goal section to be a space of four feet by eight feet within the goal line and between two parallel lines drawn at right angles to the goal line and distant two feet from either end of the goal.

XII. Upon a goal being gained, the opposite teams shall go to their own end of the tank, and the ball shall be thrown by the referee into the centre and play started as at beginning of game.

XIII. Each team shall have two judges, one at each goal line, who, upon a goal being made, shall notify the referee and announce the same.

Only in case the judges disagree shall the referee have power to decide whether a goal be fairly made or not.

XIV. The referee shall decide all fouls, and if in his opinion a player commits a foul he shall caution the team for the first offence and give the opponents a free trial for goal at each succeeding foul.

A free trial for goal will be given by lining up three backs of the defending team within the 4-foot line and giving three forwards of the opposing team the ball on the 15-foot line, when they may try for a goal until a goal is scored or the ball goes outside the 15-foot line. Only three men from each side will be allowed within the 15-foot line, until the ball goes outside that line or a goal is scored.

Fouls.—It shall be a foul to tackle an opponent if the ball is not within four feet of him or to hold him by any part of his costume. It shall be a foul to cross the 4-foot line ahead of the ball, unless forced over by an opponent, or to hang on to the sides of the tank except for the purpose of resting.

Unnecessary rough work may, within the discrimination of the referee, either be counted a foul or the referee may put the offender out of the tank until a goal is scored or the half ends.

OFFICIAL RULES FOR ALL ATHLETIC SPORTS.

The following list contains the Group and the Number of the book of Spalding's Athletic Library in which the rules wanted are contained. See front pages of book for com lete list of Spalding's Athletic Library.

EVENT.	Group	No.	EVENT.	Group	No.
All-Round Athletic Championship	12	182	Lawn Bowls	11	207
A. A. U. Athletic Rules	12	311	Lawn Games	11	188
A. A. U. Boxing Rules	12	311	Lawn Tennis	4	4
A. A. U. Gymnastic Rules	12	311	Obstacle Races	12	55
A. A. U. Water Polo Rules	12	311	Olympic Game Events—Marathon Race, Stone Throwing with Impetus, Spear Throwing, Hellenic Method of Throwing Discus, Discus, Greek Style for Youths	12	55
A. A. U. Wrestling Rules	12	311			
Archery	11	248			
Badminton	11	188			
Base Ball	1	1			
Indoor	9	9	Pigeon Flying	12	55
Basket Ball, Official	7	7	Pin Ball	12	55
Collegiate	7	312	Playground Ball	1	306
Women's	7	318	Polo (Equestrian)	10	19?
Water	12	55	Polo, Rugby	12	55
Basket Goal	6	188	Polo, Water (A. A. U.)	12	311
Bat Ball	12	55	Potato Racing	12	311
Betting	12	55	Professional Racing, Sheffield Rules	12	55
Bowling	8	8			
Boxing—A. A. U., Marquis of Queensbury, London Prize Ring	14	162	Public Schools Athletic League Athletic Rules	12	313
			Girls' Branch; including Rules for School Games	12	314
Broadsword (mounted)	12	55			
Caledonian Games	12	55	Push Ball	11	170
Canoeing	13	23	Push Ball, Water	12	55
Children's Games	11	189	Quoits	11	167
Court Tennis	11	194	Racquets	11	194
Cricket	3	3	Revolver Shooting	12	55
Croquet	11	138	Ring Hockey	6	180
Curling	11	14	Roller Polo	10	10
Dog Racing	12	55	Roller Skating Rink	10	10
Fencing	14	165	Roque	11	271
Foot Ball	2	2	Rowing	13	128
Code of Rules	2	334	Sack Racing	12	55
Association (Soccer)	2	2A	Shuffleboard	12	55
English Rugby	12	55	Skating	13	209
Canadian	2	332	Skittles	12	55
Golf	5	5	Snowshoeing	12	55
Golf-Croquet	6	188	Squash Racquets	11	194
Hand Ball	11	13	Swimming	13	177
Hand Polo	10	188	Tether Tennis	11	188
Hand Tennis	11	194	Three-Legged Race	12	55
Hitch and Kick	12	55	Volley Ball	6	188
Hockey	6	304	Wall Scaling	12	55
Ice	6	6	Walking	12	55
Field	6	154	Water Polo (American)	12	311
Garden	6	188	Water Polo (English)	12	55
Lawn	6	188	Wicket Polo	10	188
Parlor	6	188	Wrestling	14	236
Ring	12	55	Y. M. C. A. All-Round Test	12	302
Ontario Hockey Ass'n	6	256	Y. M. C. A. Athletic Rules	12	302
Indoor Base Ball	9	9	Y. M. C. A. Hand Ball Rules	12	302
Intercollegiate A. A. A. A.	12	307	Y.M.C.A. Pentathlon Rules	12	302
I.-C. Gymnastic Ass'n	15	333	Y.M.C.A. Volley Ball Rules	12	302
Lacrosse	11	201			
U. S. I.-C. Lacrosse League	11	337			

ACCEPT NO SUBSTITUTE — THE SPALDING TRADE-MARK GUARANTEES QUALITY

Spalding Rubber Quoits

No. 5. These quoits are of durable quality and should not be compared to the many worthless imitations whose only recommendation is cheapness. Made of best Para rubber. For indoor or outdoor use. Four quoits to a set. . Set, $2.00

Spalding Loaded Rubber Quoits

No. 6. Will not slide or roll. Weigh about 5 lbs. to a set. Specially adapted for indoor use. Four to a set. . . . . . . Per set, $3.00

Spalding Indoor Quoit Pins

No. J. Made with floor plate and detachable pin, which can be unscrewed when not in use, leaving plate flush with floor. . . . Per pair, 75c.

Spalding Japanned Iron Quoits

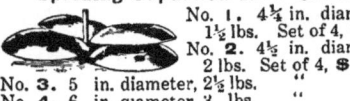

No. 1. 4¼ in. diameter. 1½ lbs. Set of 4, 60c.
No. 2. 4½ in. diameter, 2 lbs. Set of 4, $.75
No. 3. 5 in. diameter, 2½ lbs. " .90
No. 4. 6 in. diameter, 3 lbs. " 1.25
No. W. Wrought iron pins. . . Per pair, .30

Spalding Official Quoit Pins

No. X. Steel. Measure 36 inches long by 1 inch in diameter, and are made so that referee can take measurements without difficulty. Pair, $2.00

Spalding Official Push Ball

Inflated, this ball measures six feet in diameter, and it is so constructed that there is practically no danger of puncturing. The cover is of heavy cowhide, sewn by the same workmen who have been making our foot balls and basket balls for years past. The bladder is made of pure Para rubber. This ball is really the only one that should be put in play by teams who wish to avoid disappointing their audience on account of puncture during the course of a game.
No. H. Push Ball. Complete, $300.00
No. O. Large Cylinder Foot Pump, for inflating push ball. . . . - $10.00

Spalding Official Iron Quoits

No. O. Made to conform exactly to official rules. Malleable iron, 8⅝ inches in diameter, with hand clasp, as shown in cut. . Per set of 4, $10.00

Spalding Quoit Game

No. Q. Metal stand, with nickel-plated upright pin and six gutta percha quoits. An interesting game for indoors, as the quoits will not mar furniture or woodwork.
Complete, $3.00
No. QR. Rings. . . 20c. Each, 25c.

Spalding Water Polo Ball

Made of white rubber fabric. Inflated with key. Regulation size. Each, $2.50
Water Polo Guide — Containing directions for playing; official rules. 7c.
No. 129. . Each, 10c.
See Page 48 for Caps and Suits for Water Polo

Spalding Volley Ball

Volley Ball is a game which is pre-eminently fitted for the gymnasium or the exercise hall, but which may be played out of doors. The play consists of keeping the ball in motion over a high net, from one side to the other, thus partaking of the character of two games, tennis and hand ball. Balls are made of white leather. Constructed with capless ends and furnished with pure gum guaranteed bladder. Regulation size.
No. V. Best quality. . . Each, $4.00
No. W. Good quality. . . 2.50
No. A. Guaranteed Pure Para Rubber Bladder, for either Nos. V or W Volley Ball. Each, $1.00

Spalding Volley Ball Net and Standards

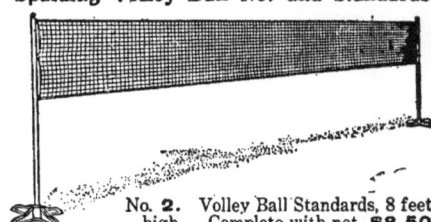

No. 2. Volley Ball Standards, 8 feet high. Complete with net, $8.50

PROMPT ATTENTION GIVEN TO ANY COMMUNICATIONS ADDRESSED TO US

A. G. SPALDING & BROS.
STORES IN ALL LARGE CITIES

FOR COMPLETE LIST OF STORES SEE INSIDE FRONT COVER OF THIS BOOK

Prices in effect January 5, 1910. Subject to change without notice. For Canadian prices see special Canadian Catalogue.

ACCEPT NO SUBSTITUTE · THE SPALDING TRADE-MARK GUARANTEES QUALITY

No. 3R   No. 2R

Spalding Patent Combination Swimming Suit

Trunks of No. 3R

Shirt of No. 3R

Best quality worsted. Furnished in solid color only. Black, Navy Blue and Gray. Shirt has combination supporter. Arm holes extra large and fastens to trunks at side with invisible catches, making a tight fitting neat combination. White canvas belt with adjustable buckle forms part of trunks, no drawing tape to knot or break. Pocket for change, etc., inside of trunks. A thoroughly up-to-date and comfortable swimming suit. No. 3R. Suit, $5.00

Expert Racing and Swimming Suits

No. 2R. Mercerized cotton, Navy Blue, silky finish, and sheds water readily; buttons over shoulders. Suit, $2.00
No. 1R. Cotton, Navy Blue, light in weight, snug fitting. Buttons over shoulders. Suit, $1.00

Spalding One-Piece Bathing Suits

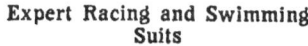

No. 743. Men's sizes, 32 to 44 inch chest; fancy stripes; button in front   SUIT 75c.
No. 521B. Boys' sizes, 24 to 32 inch chest; fancy stripes; button in front;   50c.
No. 50. Sleeveless, cotton; solid Navy Blue; button at shoulders.   75c.

Spalding Worsted Bathing Trunks

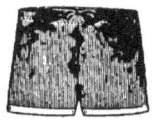

No. 1. Worsted, full fashioned, best quality, in Navy, Black, White and Maroon. $2.50
No. 2. Cut worsted, in Navy and Black. $1.25

Flannel Bathing Knee Pants

No. F. Good quality Gray or Navy flannel knee pants; fly front; belt loops. Loose fitting and just the thing for those who dislike bathing tights. $2.00

Cotton Bathing Trunks

No. 601.   Navy Blue; Red or White stripes. Per pair, 50c.
No. 602.   Solid Navy Blue.   Per pair, 35c.
No. 603.   Fancy stripes. Per pair, 25c.

Spalding Bathing Slippers

No. 13. White canvas. With soles to give protection to the feet. Any Size.   Per pair, 50c.

Spalding Waterproof Canvas Bag

No. 1. Made of canvas, lined with rubber, and thoroughly waterproof   Each, $1.00

Official Association Water Polo Cap

No. WPC. Used to distinguish swimmers in match races, the caps being made in a variety of colors. Also add interest to water polo games by enabling spectators to pick out easily the players on opposing teams.   Each, $1.00

Everfloat Swimming Collars and Jackets

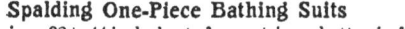

Surf Riding with Inflated Collar.

PATENTED Solid Blocks

Inflated Style Ready for Use.

No. E. An inflated collar, made with waterproof canvas outer cover, and fine quality rubber inner tube for inflation. Complete with canvas straps to go under arms and over shoulders. A most reliable, simple and quickly adjusted swimming collar and life preserver. Can be used also as boat seat, etc. Inflated Collar.   Each, $3.00
No. N. This jacket is filled with solid blocks of indurated fibre, more buoyant and reliable than ordinary cork jackets. Complete with canvas straps to go under arms and over shoulders. Solid Jacket.   Each, $3.00

Spalding Cork Swimming Jackets and Collars These jackets and collars are covered with a close woven waterproof canvas and stuffed with ground cork. No. 1. Jacket for adults, weight 2¼ lbs. Ea., $2.00
No. 2. Jacket for children, weight 1½ lbs. Ea., $1.75 | No. 3. Collars for adults or children.   1.00
Ayvad's Water Wings No. 1. Plain white. Each, 25c. | No. 2. Variegated colors. Each, 35c.

| PROMPT ATTENTION GIVEN TO ANY COMMUNICATIONS ADDRESSED TO US | A. G. SPALDING & BROS. STORES IN ALL LARGE CITIES | FOR COMPLETE LIST OF STORES SEE INSIDE FRONT COVER OF THIS BOOK |

Prices in effect January 5, 1910. Subject to change without notice. For Canadian prices see special Canadian Catalogue.

ACCEPT NO SUBSTITUTE THE SPALDING TRADE-MARK GUARANTEES QUALITY

Spalding Two Piece Bathing Suits
ALL STYLES FURNISHED IN SIZES 28 TO 44 INCH CHEST MEASUREMENT

No. 605.   No. 606.   No. 28   No. 396   No. 396B   No. 195

No. 605. Sleeveless, cotton, Navy Blue. Suit. **75c.**

No. 606. Sleeveless, cotton, in Navy Blue, with either Red or White trimmings on shirt; plain pants. . . . Per suit, **$1.00**

No. 608. Sleeveless, finest quality cotton, trimmed pants and shirts. Colors: Navy and Red or Navy and White only. . Per suit, **$1.25**

No. 28. Quarter sleeve, cotton, fashioned, mercerized silk trimming in following colors only: Navy trimmed Red; Navy trimmed White. Suit **$1.50**

No. 600. Fine quality cut worsted, in plain Navy, Black or Maroon; sleeveless style. Per suit **$3.00**

No. 601. Fine quality cut worsted in plain Navy, Black and Maroon; quarter sleeve. Suit **$3.25**

No. 396. Sleeveless, fine quality worsted, with plain pants, either Black or Navy Blue, and shirt striped two inches each color alternately in following combinations: Red and Black, Red and White, Navy and Red, Black and Orange, Cardinal and Gray, Royal Blue and White, Maroon and White. Per suit, **$3.50**

No. 396B. Sleeveless, fine quality worsted, with plain pants, either Black or Navy Blue, and shirt with 4-inch stripe around body in following combinations: Navy and White, Black and Orange, Black and Red, Gray and Cardinal. . Per suit, **$3.50**

No. 195. Sleeveless, fancy worsted, with attractive striping on shirt and pants in following colors: Black trimmed Red; Navy trimmed Gray; Gray trimmed Navy; Navy trimmed White. Suit, **$3.50**

No. 614. Quarter sleeve, fine quality worsted, striping on shirt and pants in following colors only: Navy trimmed Gray; Navy trimmed White; Gray trimmed Navy; Navy trimmed Red. . Per suit, **$3.75**

No. 196. "V" Neck, sleeveless, fancy worsted, with striping on shirt and pants in following colors only: Black trimmed Red; Navy trimmed Gray; Gray trimmed Navy; Navy trimmed White. Suit, **$4.00**

No. 110. Sleeveless, worsted, full fashioned, best quality, Navy, Black or Maroon. . Suit, **$5.00**

No. 111. Quarter sleeve, striped worsted, same quality as No. 110, in following colors only: Maroon trimmed White; Black trimmed Orange; Navy trimmed white. . Per suit, **$5.50**

No. 95. "V" Neck, sleeveless, light weight sweater yarn, solid colors; trimmings of different color in following combinations: Gray and Navy, Navy and White, Black and Light Blue. Per suit, **$5.50**

No. 295. Sleeveless, extra quality fashioned worsted, with attractive striping on shirt and pants in following colors: Gray trimmed Navy; Navy trimmed Gray; Navy trimmed White. Per suit, **$6.00**

No. 614   No. 196   No. 110   No. 111   No. 95   No. 295

PROMPT ATTENTION GIVEN TO ANY COMMUNICATIONS ADDRESSED TO US   **A. G. SPALDING & BROS.**   **FOR COMPLETE LIST OF STORES SEE INSIDE FRONT COVER OF THIS BOOK**
STORES IN ALL LARGE CITIES

Prices in effect January 5, 1910. Subject to change without notice. For Canadian prices see special Canadian Catalogue

ACCEPT NO SUBSTITUTE — THE SPALDING TRADE-MARK GUARANTEES QUALITY

SPALDING *Automobile* SWEATER

Collar Turned Up

Collar Turned Down

No. **WJ.** Most satisfactory and comfortable style for automobilists; also useful for training purposes, reducing weight, tramping during cold weather, golfing, shooting, tobogganing, snowshoeing; in fact, for every purpose where a garment is required to give protection from cold or inclement weather. High collar that may be turned down, changing it into neatest form of button front sweater. Highest quality special heavy worsted. Sizes, 28 to 44 inches. In stock colors. Each, **$8.50**

PLAIN COLORS—All Spalding Sweaters are supplied in any of the colors designated, at regular prices. Other colors to order only in any quality, 50c. each garment extra.
SPECIAL NOTICE—We will furnish any of the solid color sweaters with one color body and another color (not striped) collar and cuffs in stock colors only at no extra charge.
N. B.—We designate three shades which are sometimes called RED: These are Scarlet, Cardinal and Maroon. Where RED is specified on order Scarlet will be supplied.

STOCK COLORS

Gray	Navy	Pink
Orange	Royal Blue	Purple
Black	Columbia Blue	Yellow
White	Peacock Blue	Seal Brown
Maroon	Dark Green	Old Gold
Scarlet	Olive Green	Drab
Cardinal	Irish Green	

Spalding "Highest Quality" Sweaters

We allow four inches for stretch in all our sweaters, and sizes are marked accordingly. It is suggested, however, that for very heavy men a size about two inches larger than coat measurement be ordered to insure a comfortable fit.

WORSTED SWEATERS. Made of special quality wool, and exceedingly soft and pleasant to wear. They are full fashioned to body and arms and put together by hand, not simply stitched up on a machine as are the majority of garments sold as regular made goods.

All made with 9-inch collars; sizes 28 to 44 inches.

No. **AA.** The proper style for use after heavy exercise, inducing copious perspiration, for reducing weight or getting into condition for athletic contests. Particularly suitable also for Foot Ball and Skating. Heaviest sweater made. In stock colors. Each, **$9.00**
No. **A.** "Intercollegiate." In stock colors. Special weight. **7.00**
No. **B.** Heavy weight. In stock colors. **6.00**

Shaker Sweater

In Stock Colors. Sizes 30 to 44 in.

Fills a demand for as heavy a weight as our "Highest Quality" grade, but at a lower price.
No. **3.** Standard weight, slightly lighter than No. B. Each, **$4.00**

Spalding Vest Collar Sweater

Spalding Combined Knitted Muffler and Chest Protector

Front View   Back View

No. **M.** Special weight; highest quality worsted in solid stock colors to match our sweaters. Each, **$1.25**

PRICES SUBJECT TO CHANGE WITHOUT NOTICE

No. **BG.** Best quality worsted, good weight; with extreme open or low neck. In stock colors. Ea., **$6.00**

PROMPT ATTENTION GIVEN TO ANY COMMUNICATIONS ADDRESSED TO US

A. G. SPALDING & BROS.
STORES IN ALL LARGE CITIES

FOR COMPLETE LIST OF STORES SEE INSIDE FRONT COVER OF THIS BOOK

Prices in effect January 5, 1910. Subject to change without notice. For Canadian prices see special Canadian Catalogue.

ACCEPT NO SUBSTITUTE THE SPALDING TRADE-MARK **GUARANTEES QUALITY**

SPALDING JACKET SWEATERS

STOCK COLORS — PLAIN COLORS—All Spalding Sweaters are supplied in any of the following stock colors at regular prices. Other colors to order only in any quality 50c. each extra.

GRAY	WHITE	CARDINAL	COLUMBIA BLUE	OLIVE GREEN	PURPLE	OLD GOLD
ORANGE	MAROON	NAVY BLUE	PEACOCK BLUE	IRISH GREEN	YELLOW	DRAB
BLACK	SCARLET	ROYAL BLUE	DARK GREEN	PINK	SEAL BROWN	

SPECIAL NOTICE—We will furnish any of the solid color sweaters mentioned below with one color body and another color (not striped) collar and cuffs in stock colors only at no extra charge. This does not apply to the No. 3JB Boys' Sweater.

Sizes 28 to 44 inch chest measurement. We allow four inches for stretch in all our sweaters, and sizes are marked accordingly. It is suggested, however, that for very heavy men a size about two inches larger than coat measurement be ordered to insure a comfortable fit.

BUTTON FRONT

No. VG. Best quality worsted, heavy weight, pearl buttons. Made in regular stock colors, also in Dark Brown Mixture. Each, **$7.00**

No. DJ. Fine worsted, standard weight, pearl buttons, fine knit edging. Made in regular stock colors, also in Sage Gray. Each, **$6.00**

No. 3J. Standard weight wool, Shaker knit, pearl buttons. In stock colors. Each, **$5.00**

WITH POCKETS

No. VGP. Best quality worsted, heavy weight, pearl buttons. In stock colors. With pocket on either side and a particularly convenient and popular style for golf players. Each, **$7.50**

No. VG. Showing special trimmed edging and cuffs supplied, if desired, on jacket sweaters at no extra charge.

No. VGP

Spalding Special Base Ball Sweaters

No. CDW. Good quality worsted, ribbed knit. In stock colors. Special trimmed edging and cuffs in stock colors supplied at no extra charge. Each, **$5.50**

Boys' Jacket Sweater

No. 3JB. This is an all wool jacket sweater, with pearl buttons; furnished only in sizes from 30 to 36 inches chest measurement. In stock colors. Each, **$3.50**

Spalding Ladies' Sweaters

Knit in the Spalding athletic stitch of best quality long fibre worsted; full fashioned to shape of body on special machine and finished by hand. Cuffs, pocket and edging of special stitch. Good quality pearl buttons. Patch pockets. Attractive in appearance and, being properly made, they fit well and give satisfactory wear. Furnished in regular stock colors.

No. LDJ. Ladies' Sweater, regular button front. Each, **$8.00**

No. LWJ. With special reversible collar, as on our Men's No. WJ Automobile Sweater. Each, **$10.00**

No. CDW

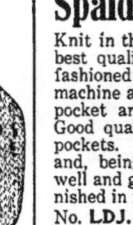
No. 3JB

| PROMPT ATTENTION GIVEN TO ANY COMMUNICATIONS ADDRESSED TO US | **A. G. SPALDING & BROS.** STORES IN ALL LARGE CITIES | FOR COMPLETE LIST OF STORES SEE INSIDE FRONT COVER OF THIS BOOK |

Prices in effect January 5, 1910. Subject to change without notice. For Canadian prices see special Canadian Catalogue.

ACCEPT NO SUBSTITUTE — THE SPALDING TRADE-MARK GUARANTEES QUALITY

Spalding New and Improved Worsted Jerseys

Following sizes carried in stock regularly in all qualities: 28 to 44 inch chest. Other sizes at an advanced price.

We allow two inches for stretch in all our Jerseys, and sizes are marked accordingly. It is suggested, however, that for very heavy men a size about two inches larger than coat measurement be ordered to insure a comfortable fit.

STOCK COLORS — PLAIN COLORS—The following stock colors are supplied in our worsted jerseys (NOT Nos. 6 or 6X) at regular prices. Other colors to order only in any quality (EXCEPT Nos. 6 and 6X), 25c. each extra.

Gray	Scarlet	Peacock Blue	Purple
Orange	Cardinal	Dark Green	Yellow
Black	Navy Blue	Olive Green	Seal Brown
White	Royal Blue	Irish Green	Old Gold
Maroon	Columbia Blue	Pink	Drab

No. 1P. Full regular made; that is, fashioned or knit to exact shape on the machine and then put together by hand, altogether different from cutting them out of a piece of material and sewing them up on a machine as are the majority of garments known as Jerseys. Special quality worsted. Solid stock colors. . . . . Each, **$4.50**

No. 10P. Worsted, fashioned. Solid stock colors, Each, **$3.00**

No. 12P. Worsted; solid stock colors. Each, **$2.75**

No. 12XB. Boys' Jersey. Worsted. Furnished in sizes 26 to 36 inches chest measurement only. Solid stock colors only. No special orders. Each, **$2.00**

Jerseys are being used more and more by base ball players, especially for early Spring and late Fall games. The Spalding line includes a complete assortment of styles and qualities.

Nos 1P, 10P and 12P

SPECIAL NOTICE We will furnish any of the above solid color Jerseys, (except Nos. 6 and 6X) with one color body and another color (not striped) collar and cuffs in stock colors only at no extra charge.

Spalding Cotton Jerseys

No. 6. Cotton, good quality, fashioned, roll collar, full length sleeves. Colors: Black, Navy Blue, Gray and Maroon only. Each, **$1.00**

No. 6X. Cotton, same as No. 6, but with striped sleeves in following combinations only: Navy with White or Red stripe; Black with Orange or Red stripe; Maroon with White stripe. . Each, **$1.25**

Woven Letters, Numerals or Designs

We weave into our best grade Jerseys, No. 1P, Letters, Numerals and Designs in special colors as desired. Prices quoted on application. Designs submitted.

PRICES SUBJECT TO ADVANCE WITHOUT NOTICE

PROMPT ATTENTION GIVEN TO ANY COMMUNICATIONS ADDRESSED TO US — **A. G. SPALDING & BROS.** STORES IN ALL LARGE CITIES — FOR COMPLETE LIST OF STORES SEE INSIDE FRONT COVER OF THIS BOOK

Prices in effect January 5, 1910. Subject to change without notice. For Canadian prices see special Canadian Catalogue.

ACCEPT NO SUBSTITUTE THE SPALDING TRADE-MARK GUARANTEES QUALITY

Spalding Coat Jerseys

Following sizes carried in stock regularly in all qualities: 28 to 44 inch chest. Other sizes at an advanced price.

We allow two inches for stretch in all our Jerseys, and sizes are marked accordingly. It is suggested, however, that for very heavy men a size about two inches larger than coat measurement be ordered to insure a comfortable fit.

STOCK COLORS

| Gray | Black | Maroon | Cardinal | Royal Blue | Peacock Blue | Olive Green | Pink | Yellow | Old Gold |
| Orange | White | Scarlet | Navy | Columbia Blue | Dark Green | Irish Green | Purple | Seal Brown | Drab |

PLAIN COLORS—The above stock colors are supplied in our worsted Jerseys (NOT Nos. 6 or 6X) at regular prices. Other colors to order only in any quality (EXCEPT Nos. 6 or 6X) 25c. each extra.

STRIPES AND TRIMMINGS—Supplied as specified in any of the above stock colors (not more than two colors in any garment) at regular prices. Other colors to order only in any quality (EXCEPT Nos. 6 or 6X) 25c. each extra.

Nos. 10C and 12C

No. 10CP

The Spalding Coat Jerseys are made of the same worsted yarn from which we manufacture our better grade Jerseys, Nos. 10P and 12P, and no pains have been spared to turn them out in a well made and attractive manner. Plain solid stock colors (not striped) or one solid stock color body and sleeves with different stock color solid trimming (not striped) on cuffs, collar and front edging. Pearl buttons.

No. **10C.** Same grade as our No. 10P.   Each, **$3.50**
No. **12C.** Same grade as our No. 12P.   Each, **$3.00**
No. **10CP.** Pockets, otherwise same as No. 10C.   Each, **$4.25**

Spalding Striped and V-Neck Jerseys

Note list of stock colors above

Nos. 10PW and 12PW

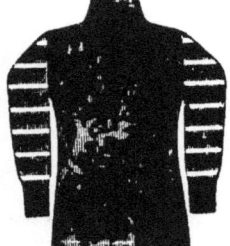

Nos. 10PX and 12PX

No. 12PV

No. **10PW.** Good quality worsted, same grade as No. 10P. Solid stock color body and sleeves, with 6-inch stock color stripe around body.   Each, **$3.50**

No. **12PW.** Worsted; solid stock color body and sleeves with 6-inch stock color stripe around body.   Each, **$3.00**

No. **10PX.** Good quality worsted, fashioned; solid stock color body, with stock color striped sleeves, usually alternating two inches of same color as body, with narrow stripes of any other stock color.   Each, **$3.50**

No. **12PV** Worsted, solid stock colors, with V-neck instead of full collar as on regular jerseys.   Each, **$3.00**

No. **12PX.** Worsted, solid stock color body, with stock color striped sleeves, usually alternating two inches of same color as body, with narrow stripes of any other stock color.   Each, **$3.00**

PRICES SUBJECT TO CHANGE WITHOUT NOTICE

| PROMPT ATTENTION GIVEN TO ANY COMMUNICATIONS ADDRESSED TO US | **A. G. SPALDING & BROS.** STORES IN ALL LARGE CITIES | FOR COMPLETE LIST OF STORES SEE INSIDE FRONT COVER OF THIS BOOK |

Prices in effect January 5, 1910. Subject to change without notice. For Canadian prices see special Canadian Catalogue.

ACCEPT NO SUBSTITUTE — THE SPALDING TRADE-MARK GUARANTEES QUALITY

STOCK COLORS	Gray	Orange	Black	Royal Blue	Pink
			White	Columbia Blue	Purple
			Maroon	Peacock Blue	Yellow
			Scarlet	Dark Green	Seal Brown
			Cardinal	Olive Green	Old Gold
			Navy	Irish Green	Drab

PLAIN COLORS—All Spalding Stockings are supplied in any of the colors designated, at regular prices. Other colors to order only in any quality except No. 4R, 25c. per pair extra.

STRIPES—Striped Stockings are supplied in any of the colors noted (not more than two colors) at regular prices. Other colors to order only in any quality except No. 4RC, 25c. per pair extra.

N.B.—We designate three shades which are sometimes called RED: These are Scarlet, Cardinal and Maroon. Where RED is specified on order Scarlet will be supplied.

Spalding Stockings

Our "Highest Quality" Stockings are best quality worsted, have white mercerized cotton feet, are heavy ribbed, full fashioned, hug the leg closely but comfortably, and are very durable.

No. 3-O. Plain stock colors, best worsted, white mercerized feet. . . . . . Pair, $1.50
No. 3-OS. Alternate striped, stock colors, best quality worsted, white mercerized feet. Pair, $1.75
No. 3-OC. Calf with one stripe 4 in. wide, stock colors, best quality worsted, white mercerized feet. Pr., $1.75

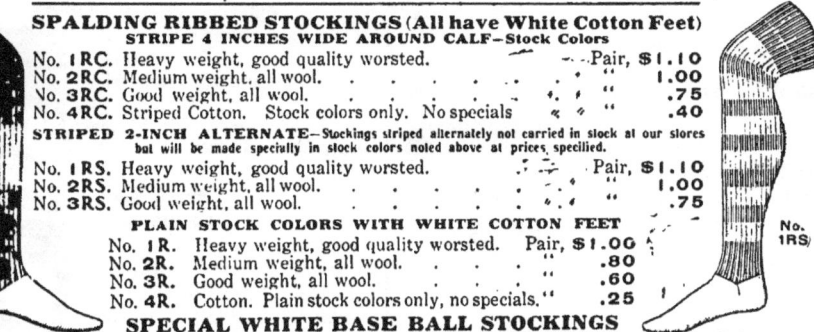

SPALDING RIBBED STOCKINGS (All have White Cotton Feet)
STRIPE 4 INCHES WIDE AROUND CALF—Stock Colors

No. 1RC. Heavy weight, good quality worsted. . . . Pair, $1.10
No. 2RC. Medium weight, all wool. . . . . " 1.00
No. 3RC. Good weight, all wool. . . . . " .75
No. 4RC. Striped Cotton. Stock colors only. No specials . . .40

STRIPED 2-INCH ALTERNATE—Stockings striped alternately not carried in stock at our stores but will be made specially in stock colors noted above at prices specified.

No. 1RS. Heavy weight, good quality worsted. . . . Pair, $1.10
No. 2RS. Medium weight, all wool. . . . . " 1.00
No. 3RS. Good weight, all wool. . . . . " .75

PLAIN STOCK COLORS WITH WHITE COTTON FEET

No. 1R. Heavy weight, good quality worsted. Pair, $1.00
No. 2R. Medium weight, all wool. . . . " .80
No. 3R. Good weight, all wool. . . . " .60
No. 4R. Cotton. Plain stock colors only, no specials. " .25

SPECIAL WHITE BASE BALL STOCKINGS

No. BB. Natural white stockings, light weight, to be worn under regular colored stockings. Pair, 15c.

SPALDING LEATHER BELTS

No. 805. Genuine pigskin, hand made. Nickel buckle. Each, 25c.
No. 804. Hand made, 1¼ inch, black leather. Nickeled harness buckle. Each, $1.00
No. 803. Hogskin leather. Light tan color. Nickeled buckle. Each, $1.00
No. 808. Hand made. 1¼ inch black leather. Brass harness buckle. Each, $1.00
No. 807. Black bridle leather, ⅞ inch wide. Brass harness buckle. Each, 75c.

No. 806. Black leather, ⅝ in. wide. Black harness buckle. Each, 75c.
No. 802. Buff or Brown leather, lined with patent leather, 1¼ inch wide. Each, 75c.
No. 801. Fine 1½ inch leather belt. Black or Tan. Heavy harness buckle. Each, 60c.
No. 800. Tan or Black leather belt. 1¼ inch wide. Fine harness buckle. Each, 60c.
No. 725. 1¼ inch heavy leather, heavy nickeled harness buckle. Colors: Tan, Orange or Black. Each, 50c.
No. 754. 1¼ inch nickel harness buckle. Colors: Tan or Orange. Each, 40c.

Spalding "Special" Leather Base Ball Belt

No. 400. This black leather 1¾-inch belt is specially shaped for athletic use, particularly base ball. Heavy harness buckle. Each, 75c.

Worsted Web Belts—Colors: Red, Royal Blue, Navy Blue, Black, White, Maroon
No. 3-O. Special League Belt, leather lined; large nickel-plated buckle. Each, $1.00
No. 2. Worsted Belt, with two metal buckles. . .50
No. 47. Worsted Belt, with one leather covered buckle. .50

Spalding Cotton Web Belts—Colors: Red, White, Royal Blue, Maroon, Navy Blue
No. 23. Cotton Belt, two metal buckles. Each, 35c. | No. 4. Cotton Belt, one metal buckle. Each, 25c.
No. 5. Cotton Belt. Each, 10c.

PROMPT ATTENTION GIVEN TO ANY COMMUNICATIONS ADDRESSED TO US — **A. G. SPALDING & BROS.** STORES IN ALL LARGE CITIES — FOR COMPLETE LIST OF STORES SEE INSIDE FRONT COVER OF THIS BOOK

Prices in effect January 5, 1910. Subject to change without notice. For Canadian prices see special Canadian Catalogue.

ACCEPT NO SUBSTITUTE THE SPALDING TRADE-MARK **GUARANTEES QUALITY**

Spalding Elastic Supporters

No. 2. Best Canton flannel, with elastic pieces on side. . . Each, **50c.**

No. 3. Like No. 2, but open mesh front. Each, **50c.**

Spalding All Elastic Supporter (Black)

Made of good quality black covered elastic. Waistband six inches wide. Furnished in small, medium and large.

No. DX. Each, **$1.25**

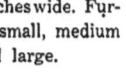

Spalding Supporters

No. 1. Best Canton flannel, one in box. Each, **25c.**
No. X. Same as No. 1 but cheaper in quality **20c.**

No. A. Swimming Supporter. For water polo, bathing and swimming. Buttons at side and fitted with draw-string. Each, **50c.**

Spalding Suspensories

THE "SPALDING" STYLE

No. 70. Non-elastic bands, knitted sack. Each, **25c.**
No. 71. Elastic buttock bands, knitted sack. Each, **35c.**
No. 72. Elastic bands, knitted sack. Each, **50c.**
No. 73½. Elastic bands, silk sack. Each, **75c.**
No. 76. Silk bands, finest silk sack. Each, **$1.25**

"OLD POINT COMFORT" STYLE

No. 2. Lisle thread sack. Each, **$1.00**
No. 3. Fine silk sack, satin trimmings. Each, **$1.25**
No. 4. Silk bands, satin trimmings, finest silk sack. Each, **$1.50**

BIKE JOCKEY STRAP SUSPENSORY

For athletes, base ball, foot ball, tennis players, etc. All elastic; no buckles. Three sizes: Small, to fit waist 22 to 28 inches; Medium, 30 to 38 inches; Large, 40 to 48 inches. No. 5. Each, **75c.**

Pat. Nov. 30, 1897

SPECIAL COMBINATION SUSPENSORY (ALL ELASTIC)

Made of same material as in the regular Bike Suspensory, but with waist-band eight inches wide, providing additional support needed during rigid training and athletic contests. Sizes: Small, 22 to 28 inches; Medium, 30 to 38 inches; Large, 40 to 48 inches. No. B6. Each, **$1.50**

Spalding Leather Abdomen Protector

Heavy sole leather, well padded with quilted lining and non-elastic bands, with buckles at side and elastic at back. For boxing, hockey, foot ball, etc. No other supporter necessary with this style.
No. S Each, **$3.00**

Spalding Aluminum Abdomen Protector

Pat. April 9 1907

Aluminum, edges well padded with rubber. Elastic cross bands and belt.
No. 3. Each, **$3.50**

Spalding Wire Abdomen Protector

Heavy wire, well padded with wool fleece and chamois. Leather belt, straps for fastening. Used with any of our regular supporters or suspensories.
No. 4. Each, **$2.00**

PROMPT ATTENTION GIVEN TO ANY COMMUNICATIONS ADDRESSED TO US — **A. G. SPALDING & BROS.** STORES IN ALL LARGE CITIES — FOR COMPLETE LIST OF STORES SEE INSIDE FRONT COVER OF THIS BOOK

Prices in effect January 5, 1910. Subject to change without notice. For Canadian prices see special Canadian Catalogue.

ACCEPT NO SUBSTITUTE — THE SPALDING TRADE-MARK GUARANTEES QUALITY

Spalding Leather Wrist Supporters

No. 50

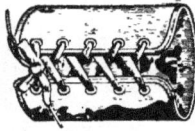
No. 300

No. 400

No. 50. Grain leather, lined, single strap-and-buckle. Each, 20c.

No. 100. Solid belt leather, tan or black, single strap-and-buckle. Each, 25c.

No. 200. Solid belt leather, tan or black, double strap-and-buckle. Each, 40c.

No. 200

No. 300. Solid belt leather, tan or black, laced fastening. Each, 25c.

No. 400. Genuine pigskin, lined, in improved English slitted style. Each, 50c.

Spalding Combination Foot Ball Glove and Wrist Supporter

Pat. June 17, 1902

Designed by H. B. Conibear. Back of hand protected by a piece of sole leather, and any strain to wrist is avoided by leather strap supporter which forms the upper part of the glove. Made for right or left hand. **No. 1.** Each, $1.25

Knee Cap Bandage

In ordering, give circumference below knee, at knee and just above knee, and state if light or strong pressure is desired.
No. 4. Cotton thread. Each, $1.50
No. 4A. Silk thread. " 2.25

Elbow Bandage

In ordering, give circumference above and below elbow, and state if for light or strong pressure.
No. 2. Cotton thread. EACH $1.50
No. 2A. Silk thread. 2.25

Spalding Shoulder Cap Bandage

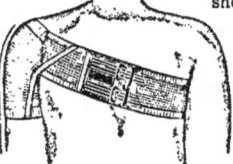

In ordering, give circumference around arm and chest. Mention for which shoulder required.

No. 1. Cotton thread. Each, $4.50
No. 1A. Silk thread. Each, $6.00

Spalding Wrist Bandage

Ankle Bandage

Give circumference around smallest part of wrist, and state whether for light or strong pressure. EACH
No. 6. Cotton thread. $ .75
No. 6A. Silk thread. 1.00

In ordering, give circumference around ankle and over instep; state if light or strong pressure is desired. EACH
No. 5. Cotton thread. $1.50
No. 5A. Silk thread. 2.25

Spalding Elastic Bandage

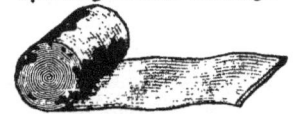

Composed of threads of rubber completely covered. Light, porous and easily applied. The pressure can be applied wherever necessary following all depressions or swellings with folding and unvarying uniformity. Quickly secured by inserting end under last fold. EACH
No. 30. Width 3 in., 5 yds. long (stretched). $1.00
No. 25. Width 2½ in., 5 yds. long (stretched). .75

Spalding Elastic Belt

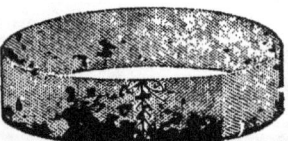

Our elastic foot ball belt stretches with the length of body and may be attached to jacket and pants, thus forming one continuous suit. By closely fitting the body, the opposing player has less chance of tackling. Allows perfect freedom in all positions.
No. 1. Width 6 inches. Each, $1.50

PROMPT ATTENTION GIVEN TO ANY COMMUNICATIONS ADDRESSED TO US

A. G. SPALDING & BROS.
STORES IN ALL LARGE CITIES

FOR COMPLETE LIST OF STORES SEE INSIDE FRONT COVER OF THIS BOOK

Prices in effect January 5, 1910. Subject to change without notice. For Canadian prices see special Canadian Catalogue.

SPALDING MASCOT PENNANTS

Made by special patented process. We use only best quality felt and other materials and guarantee work not to fade, crack or come off. Our stock includes pennants with mascots of most of the larger schools, colleges and universities in the United States and Canada—absolute reproductions in the proper colors. The complete list of schools, colleges and universities whose mascot pennants we furnish from stock is noted below:

UNIVERSITIES AND COLLEGES

ADELPHI....Foot Ball, Basket Ball	HAMILTON..........Well House	MISSOURI....Seal, Tiger Head	SYRACUSE....Crew, Seal, Foot Ball
AMHERST.....Foot Ball, Base Ball	BARVARD {Seal, Crew, Foot Ball, Mascot	MUHLENBERG...............Head	WM. SMITH..................Seal
ARMY.Seal, Cannon, Mule, Army Girl		MONTANA...{Foot Ball, Base Ball, Basket Ball	SHAW...................Foot Ball
AMES...................Foot Ball	HOBART.......Seal, Foot Ball	NORTHWESTERN.......Foot Ball	TRINITY........Mascot, Foot Ball
ARKANSAS...............Foot Ball	HOLY CROSS...........Foot Ball	NEW YORK UNIVERSITY..Foot Ball	TUFTS.................Foot Ball
BARNARD ....Basket Ball Girl	HOWARD PAYNE..Foot Ball, Track	NEBRASKA....Foot Ball, Base Ball	TULANE...............Foot Ball
BUCKNELL..............Foot Ball	ILLINOIS....Foot Ball, Base Ball	NOTRE DAME....Foot Ball, Seal	UNION....Building, Idol, Foot Ball
BRYN MAWR.........Tennis Girl	INDIANA................Foot Ball	NAVY {Crew, Battleship, Goat, Seal, Foot Ball	U. S. MILITARY {Seal, Cannon, ACADEMY Mule, Army Girl, Foot Ball
BROWN.....Bear, Seal, Foot Ball	IOWA..........Banjo Girl, Foot Ball		
BOWDOIN..............Foot Ball	IDAHO................Foot Ball	OBERLIN....Foot Ball, Base Ball	U. S. NAVAL {Crew, Battleship, ACADEMY Goat, Mascot, Seal, Foot Ball
BETHANY............Banjo Girl	KANSAS...............Foot Ball	OREGON................Foot Ball	
CALIFORNIA..........Foot Ball	KALAMAZOO...........Foot Ball	PENNSYLVANIA {Seal, Crew, Lion Head, Foot Ball	
CARLISLE..........Indian Head	LAFAYETTE..........Foot Ball		VASSAR {Basket Ball Girl, Tennis Girl
COLLEGE CITY OF N. Y..Foot Ball	LEHIGH.......Foot Ball, Base Ball	PRINCETON {Tiger Mascot, Seal, Foot Ball, Base Ball	
COLORADO.............Foot Ball	LELAND STANFORD {Crew, Foot Ball, Seal		VILLA NOVA............Foot Ball
CHICAGO....Foot Ball, Base Ball		PRATT.................Foot Ball	VIRGINIA.............Foot Ball
COLGATE..............Basket Ball	LAWRENCE {Basket Ball Girl, Foot Ball	PURDUE...............Foot Ball	VANDERBILT.........Foot Ball
COLUMBIA {Statue, Crew, Seal, Oarsman, Base Ball		POLYTECHNIC..........Mascot	WESTERN RESERVE...Foot Ball
	MAINE................Foot Ball	POMONA..............Building	WELLESLEY......Banjo Girl
CORNELL....{Crew, Foot Ball, Oarsman, Base Ball	MANHATTAN..........Foot Ball	RENSSELAER {Foot Ball, POLYTECHNIC INSTITUTE Mascot, Target	WELLS.................Seal
	MARQUETTE....Seal, Foot Ball		WESLEYAN....Foot Ball, B se Ball
CASE SCHOOL {......Foot Ball APP. SCIENCE	MICHIGAN {Athletic Colors Foot Ball Scholastic Seal Colors Foot Ball		WILLIAMS....Foot Ball, Brse Ball
CORNELL (Waterloo, Ia.)..Foot Ball		ROCHESTER.....Seal, Foot Ball	WISCONSIN..Seal, Crew, Foot Ball
COLBY................Foot Ball		RUTGERS...............Foot Ball	WASHINGTON {Foot Ball, Seal, Crew, Base Ball
DARTMOUTH..Foot Ball, Base Ball	MINNESOTA {Seal, Foot Ball, Base Ball, Basket Ball	SMITH {Seal, Basket Ball Girl, Tennis Girl	
DE PAUW.............Banjo Girl			WASHINGTON (St. Louis)..Foot Ball
FORDHAM....Foot Ball, Base Ball	MILWAUKEE-DOWNER {Basket Ball Girl	STEVENS................Foot Ball	WABASH.............Foot Ball
GEORGETOWN..Seal,Crew,Foot Ball		SWARTHMORE..........Foot Ball	YALE..Seal, Crew, Foot Ball, Mascot

PREPARATORY AND HIGH SCHOOLS

Andover......................{Foot Ball, Base Ball	East H. S. (Rochester, N. Y.)..{Building, Mascot, Foot Ball, Base Ball		Morris H. S. (New York)......Foot Ball
Boys' H. S. (Brooklyn, N. Y.).{Foot Ball, Basket Ball			Manual H. S. (St. Louis, Mo.)..Foot Ball
			Manual H. S. (Kansas City, Mo.)..Foot Ball
Boys' H. S. (New Orleans, La)..Tiger Head	Flushing H. S. (Flushing, N. Y.)...........{Foot Ball		Newark H. S. {Foot Ball, (Newark, N. J.) Basket Ball Girl
High School of Com. (N. Y.)......Foot Ball			
Central H. S. (Cleveland, O.)......Foot Ball	Girls' H. S. (B'klyn, N. Y.)..Basket Ball		Newark Academy (Newark, N. J.).Foot Ball
Clinton H. S. (New York).........Foot Ball	Gonzaga H. S. (Spokane, Wash)..Foot Ball		N. Central H. S. (Spokane, Wash.).Foot Ball
Commercial H. S. (New York)....Foot Ball	Horace Mann School (New York).Foot Ball		Pennington Academy............Foot Ball
Central H. S. (St. Louis, Mo.)....Foot Ball	Hollister H. S. (Hollister, Cal)....Building		Packer (Brooklyn, N. Y.)........Banjo Girl
Central H. S. (Kansas City, Mo.)..Foot Ball	Hosmer H. S. (St. Louis, Mo)....Foot Ball		St. Mary's (Louisville, Ky.).......Foot Ball
Erasmus (Brooklyn, N. Y.)........Foot Ball	Lawrenceville School.............Foot Ball		St. Mary's (Garden City, N. Y.) Tennis Girl
East H. S. (Cleveland, O.).......Foot Ball	Manual H. S. (New York)......Foot Ball		Technical H. S. (Buffalo, N. Y.), Buffalo Head
Englewood H. S. (Chicago).......Foot Ball	Masten Park H. S. (Buffalo, N. Y.)....Seal		Wadleigh H. S. (N. Y.)....Basket Ball Girl
			West H. S. (Cleveland, O.).......Foot Ball

SPALDING MASCOT PENNANTS No. 1. Size 15 x 36 inches. Each, $1.00
No. 3. Size 11 x 26 inches. .50

SPECIAL DESIGN ORDERS. On an order for not less than 1 GROSS. pennants of either size, No. 1 or No. 3, we will make up at regular prices special design mascot pennants with name of any school or college. When ordering enclose sample of the shade of material and the lettering and style of lettering wanted, and where special design mascot is wanted enclose a good copy, and if design is not in color state it is to be in colors and how colored.

NOTE.—For color of pennant any small piece of goods will do, felt preferred. Do not match colors at night, as they look altogether different in the daylight.

SPECIAL VARIATION ORDERS

VARIATION K—We supply on order for not less than 6 DOZEN of either size, No. 1 or No. 3, at regular prices, pennants for other schools or colleges NOT mentioned above where the mascot design is the same as on some one of our regular stock designs, the name of the school or college being special. Full particulars regarding colors, etc., should be sent on these Special Variation Orders, the same as on Special Design Orders referred to above.

VARIATION M—We also supply on orders for not less than 3 Dozen of either size, No. 1 or No. 3, at regular prices, pennants for schools, colleges or universities already on our regular stock list, but varying the design by putting on some other mascot than that which we put on regularly on the pennants for that particular school or college, the mascot design substituted being that of some other school or college on our regular stock list.

SMALLER QUANTITIES than as mentioned not supplied in Special Designs nor on Special Variation Orders.

PROMPT ATTENTION GIVEN TO ANY COMMUNICATIONS ADDRESSED TO US **A. G. SPALDING & BROS.** STORES IN ALL LARGE CITIES FOR COMPLETE LIST OF STORES SEE INSIDE FRONT COVER OF THIS BOOK

Prices in effect January 5, 1910. Subject to change without notice   For Canadian prices see special Canadian Catalogue.

THE SPALDING TRADE-MARK GUARANTEES QUALITY
ACCEPT NO SUBSTITUTE

COLLEGE, SCHOOL FLAGS AND PENNANTS

We solicit correspondence with colleges, schools, clubs and others requiring special designs or anything different from regular stock assortment as specified below.

SILK COLLEGE FLAGS in officially approved colors of the following colleges: Harvard—White H; Harvard—Black H; Yale, Princeton, Univ. of Penn., Cornell, Columbia, Univ. of Chicago, Univ. of California, Stanford Univ., Northwestern Univ., Dartmouth, Brown, Wisconsin, Univ. of New York, Georgetown Univ., Univ. of Illinois, Amherst, Univ. of Michigan, Univ. of Minnesota, Vassar, Williams.

Prices quoted below are for silk flags of the above named colleges.

No. 2. Silk Flag, 12x18 inches, good quality, oblong shape; colors and lettering printed in fast colors. Complete, mounted on ornamental staffs. . . . . Each, 50c.
No. 5. Silk Flag, 4x6 inches, oblong shape, fast colors printed, on stick. . . . " 10c.
No. 6. Cashmere Banner, size 50x70 inches, oblong shape, fine quality material, with any four 18-inch felt letters stitched on one side. . . . . Each, $5.00

COLLEGE SLEEVE BANDS
Made of any color felt, 4 inches wide and long enough to go around sleeve; with one 1½-inch letter.
Each, 25c. $2.40 Doz.
Extra letters or Numerals. Each, 5c.

FELT HAT BANDS
Made of any color felt, 1½ inches wide and long enough to go around crown of hat; with one 1-inch letter.
Each, 15c. $1.44 Doz.
Extra letters or numerals. 3c.

FELT PENNANTS
Any Solid Stock Color with regular style letters

No. 3. Felt Flag, 15x30 inches, pennant shape, one 4-inch letter stitched on each side. Complete with tapes for hanging. . Each, 50c.
No. 4. Felt Flag, 10x20 inches, pennant shape, one 3-inch letter stitched on each side. Complete with tapes for hanging. . Each, 25c.
4 inch extra letters on Felt Flag No. 3. Each, 6c.
3 inch extra letters on Felt Flag No. 4. " 5c.

PLAIN FELT PENNANTS—Any Solid Stock Color, Without Staff

With One Letter			With Any Single Name			With Any Single Name		
Any Regular	Style Letter		Plain Letters	All One Size		Graduated Letters	Any Regular Style	
	Each	Retail Doz.		Each	Retail Doz.		Each	Retail Doz.
No. 01. 9x18 in.	$ .20	$2.16	No. S1. 9x18 in.	$ .50	$4.80	No. G1. 9x18 in.	$ .65	$6.60
No. 02. 10x20 in.	.25	2.40	No. S2. 10x20 in.	.55	5.40	No. G2. 10x20 in.	.70	7.20
No. 03. 12x24 in.	.40	3.60	No. S3. 12x24 in.	.60	6.00	No. G3. 12x24 in.	.75	7.80
No. 04. 14x28 in.	.50	4.80	No. S4. 14x28 in.	.65	6.60	No. G4. 14x28 in.	.85	9.00
No. 05. 15x30 in.	.55	5.40	No. S5. 15x30 in.	.85	8.40	No. G5. 15x30 in.	1.00	10.20
No. 06. 18x36 in.	.65	6.60	No. S6. 18x36 in.	1.00	10.20	No. G6. 18x36 in.	1.25	12.00
No. 07. 36x72 in.	1.25	12.60	No. S7. 36x72 in.	1.85	19.20			

NEW WAVE PENNANTS
Felt, Stock Colors, Without Staff

		Each	Retail Doz.
No. A.	6x21 in., one letter, block style.	$ .35	$3.60
No. B.	9x23 in., one letter, with design of foot ball.	.50	4.80
No. C.	11x28 in., block letters; any single name.	.75	7.80
No. D.	11x28 in., plain letters; any single name.	.65	6.60
No. E.	14x34 in., any single name; first letter fancy.	.85	8.40
No. F.	15x36 in., any single name; first letter fancy.	.90	9.00
No. G.	15x36 in., any single name; Old English style letters.	1.10	10.80

The above prices printed in italics will be quoted on orders of one-half dozen or more at one time. No reduction from retail prices on quantities of less than one-half dozen.

PROMPT ATTENTION GIVEN TO ANY COMMUNICATIONS ADDRESSED TO US — **A. G. SPALDING & BROS. STORES IN ALL LARGE CITIES** — FOR COMPLETE LIST OF STORES SEE INSIDE FRONT COVER OF THIS BOOK

Prices in effect January 5, 1910. Subject to change without notice. — For Canadian prices see special Canadian Catalogue.

ACCEPT NO SUBSTITUTE — THE SPALDING TRADE-MARK GUARANTEES QUALITY

ATHLETIC SHIRTS, TIGHTS AND TRUNKS

STOCK COLORS AND SIZES. Worsted Goods, Best Quality. We carry following colors regularly in stock: Black, Navy Blue and Maroon, in stock sizes Shirts, 26 to 44 in. chest. Tights, 28 to 42 in. waist. Other colors and sizes made to order at special prices. Estimates on application.
Our No. 600 Line Worsted Goods. Furnished in Gray and White, Navy Blue, Maroon and Black only Stock sizes Shirts, 26 to 44 in. chest; Tights, 28 to 42 in. waist.
Sanitary Cotton Goods. Colors: Bleached White, Navy, Black, Maroon and Gray Stock sizes: 26 to 44 in. chest. Tights, 26 to 42 in. waist

Spalding Sleeveless Shirts
- No. 1E. Best Worsted, full fashioned, stock colors and sizes. Each, $3.00
- No. 600. Cut worsted, stock colors and sizes. " 1.50
- No. 6E. Sanitary Cotton, stock colors and sizes. " .50

Spalding Striped Sleeveless Shirts
- No. 600S. Cut Worsted, with 6-inch stripe around chest, in following combinations of colors; Navy with White stripe; Black with Orange stripe; Maroon with White stripe; Red with Black stripe; Royal Blue with White stripe; Black with Red stripe; Gray with Cardinal stripe. Each, $1.75
- No. 6ES. Sanitary Cotton, stock body, with 6-inch stripe around chest, in same combinations of colors as No. 600S. Each, 75c.

Spalding Shirts with Sash
- No. 6ED. Sanitary Cotton, sleeveless, solid color body with sash of different color. Same combinations of colors as No. 600S. Each, 75c.

Spalding Quarter Sleeve Shirts
- No. 1F. Best Worsted, full fashioned, stock colors and sizes. Each, $3.00
- No. 601. Cut Worsted, stock colors and sizes. " 1.75
- No. 6F. Sanitary Cotton, stock colors and sizes. " .50

Spalding Full Sleeve Shirts
- No. 3D. Cotton, Flesh, White, Black. Each, $1.00

Spalding Knee Tights
- No. 1B. Best Worsted, full fashioned, stock colors and sizes. Pair, $3.25
- No. 604. Cut Worsted, stock colors and sizes. Pair, $1.50
- No. 4B. Sanitary Cotton, stock colors and sizes. Pair, 50c.

Spalding Full Length Tights
- No. 1A. Best Worsted, full fashioned, stock colors and sizes. Pair, $4.50
- No. 605. Cut Worsted, stock colors and sizes. Pair, $2.50
- No. 3A. Cotton, full quality. White, Black, Flesh. Pair, $1.00

Spalding Running Pants
- No. 1. White or Black Sateen, fly front, lace back. Pair, $1.25
- No. 2. White or Black Sateen, fly front, lace back. Pair, $1.00
- No. 3. White or Black Silesia, fly front, lace back. Pr. 75c
- No. 4. White, Black or Gray Silesia, fly front, lace back. Pair, 50c.
- Silk Ribbon Stripes down sides of any of these running pants 25c. per pair extra
- Silk Ribbon Stripe around waist on any of these running pants 25c per pair extra.

Spalding Worsted Trunks
- No. 1. Best Worsted, Black, Maroon and Navy. Pair, $2.50
- No. 2. Cut Worsted, Navy and black. Special colors to order Pair, $1.25

Spalding Velvet Trunks
- No. 3. Fine Velvet. Colors: Black, Navy, Royal Blue, Maroon. Special colors to order. Pair, $1.00
- No. 4. Sateen. Black, White. Pair, 50c.

JUVENILE SHIRTS, TIGHTS AND PANTS
ONLY SIZES SUPPLIED—Chest, 26 to 30 inches, inclusive; Waist, 24 to 26 inches, inclusive

- No. 65. Sleeveless Shirt, quality of No. 600. $1.25 | No. 66. Quarter Sleeve Shirt, quality of No. 601. $1.50
- No. 65S. Sleeveless Shirt, quality of No. 600S 1.50 | No. 64. Knee Tights, quality of No. 604. 1.35
- No. 44. Running Pants, quality of No. 4. Pair, 45c.

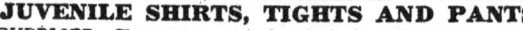

PROMPT ATTENTION GIVEN TO ANY COMMUNICATIONS ADDRESSED TO US
A. G. SPALDING & BROS.
STORES IN ALL LARGE CITIES
FOR COMPLETE LIST OF STORES SEE INSIDE FRONT COVER OF THIS BOOK

Prices in effect January 5, 1910. Subject to change without notice. For Canadian prices see special Canadian Catalogue.

ACCEPT NO SUBSTITUTE — THE SPALDING TRADE-MARK **GUARANTEES QUALITY**

Spalding Wrestling Full Tights

Best worsted, knit to shape and put together by hand. Reinforced at knees with strong silk finish worsted. Stock colors: Black, Navy Blue and Maroon. Other colors on special order. Sizes: waist, 28 to 42 inches. Larger sizes on special order. These full tights are made after the suggestions and ideas of the most prominent wrestlers, including Gotch, Oleson and others.

No. **WA.** Spalding Wrestling Full Tights. Per pair, **$6.00**

From Spalding's Athletic Library, Group XIV., No. 326. "Professional Wrestling." Price 10 cents.

Spalding Special Combined Wrestling Supporter and Belt

Mercerized silk elastic, strong and durable. The only really safe style of supporter for wrestling.

No. **WS.** Spalding Wrestling Supporter. Each, **$2.00**

No. B

Nos. 61 and 62

Spalding Special Pads for Wrestling

To be Sewn on Wrestling Tights — PAIR
No. **B.** Soft tanned horsehide cover, hair felt padding. **75c.**
No. **62.** Covered with tan leather and nicely padded. **50c.**
No. **61.** Covered with durable cloth and padded wool felt. **25c.**

Spalding Y. M. C. A. Trousers
REGULATION STYLE

No. **2.** Men's Leaders. Blue or Gray flannel, with stripe down side of leg. Per pair, **$3.50**
No. **3.** Flannel, good quality. " **3.00**
No. **4.** Flannel, medium quality. " **1.75**

Spalding Boys' Knee Pants

No. **2B.** Boys' Leaders. Blue flannel Y. M. C. A. Knee Pants, with stripe down side. Per pair, **$2.50**
No. **14B.** Boys' Knee Pants, Material same quality as No. 4 Y.M.C.A. trousers, with stripe down side. **$1.00**

PROMPT ATTENTION GIVEN TO ANY COMMUNICATIONS ADDRESSED TO US — **A. G. SPALDING & BROS.** STORES IN ALL LARGE CITIES — FOR COMPLETE LIST OF STORES SEE INSIDE FRONT COVER OF THIS BOOK

Prices in effect January 5, 1910. Subject to change without notice. For Canadian prices see special Canadian Catalogue.

ACCEPT NO SUBSTITUTE THE SPALDING TRADE-MARK **GUARANTEES QUALITY**

Spalding Long Distance Running Shoes

MARATHON "Μαραθών"

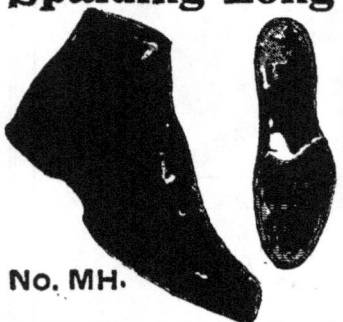

No. MH.

Made to stand up under unusual conditions—bad roads, rough, hilly and uneven, macadam, dirt, asphalt, brick or wood. Made after suggestions of men who are competing in long distance races continually under every conceivable condition.

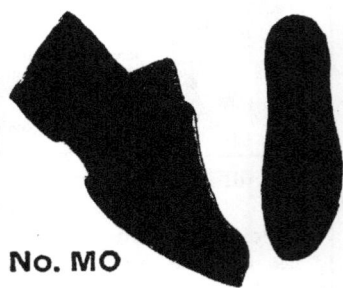

No. MO

No. **MH.** High cut. Corrugated tap rubber sole and cushioned leather heel; special quality black leather uppers. Full finished inside so as not to hurt the feet in a long race. Hand sewed. Pair, **$5.00**

No. **MO.** Low cut. Corrugated tap rubber sole and cushioned leather heel; special quality black leather uppers. Full finished inside so as not to hurt the feet in a long race. Hand sewed. Pair, **$5.00**

Built to win. The same models as used by many of the competitors in the famous **MARATHON** races at the 1908 Olympic Games, London, and in the most important distance races in this country since then.

Spalding Cross Country, Jumping and Hurdling Shoes

No. 14C

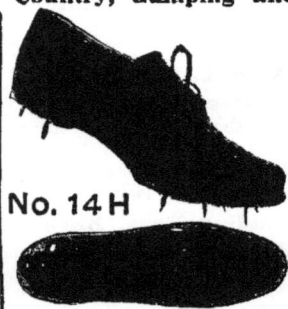

No. 14H

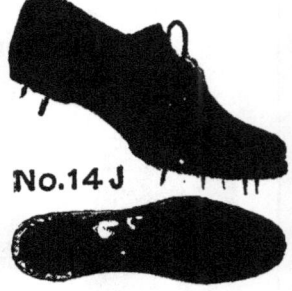

No.14J

No. **14C.** Cross Country Shoe, finest Kangaroo leather; low broad heel, flexible shank, hand sewed, six spikes on sole; with or without spikes on heel. Per pair, **$6.00**

No. **14H.** Jumping and Hurdling Shoe; fine Kangaroo leather, hand-made, specially stiffened sole; spikes in heel placed according to latest ideas to assist jumper. Pair, **$6.00**

No. **14J.** Calfskin Jumping Shoe, partly machine-made; low broad heel; spikes correctly placed. Satisfactory quality and very durable. Per pair, **$4.50**

PROMPT ATTENTION GIVEN TO ANY COMMUNICATIONS ADDRESSED TO US

A. G. SPALDING & BROS.
STORES IN ALL LARGE CITIES

FOR COMPLETE LIST OF STORES SEE INSIDE FRONT COVER OF THIS BOOK

Prices in effect January 5, 1910. Subject to change without notice. For Canadian prices see special Canadian Catalogue

ACCEPT NO SUBSTITUTE — THE SPALDING TRADE-MARK GUARANTEES QUALITY

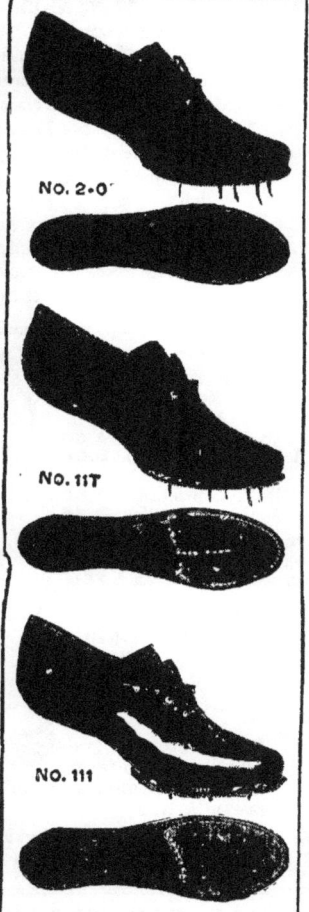

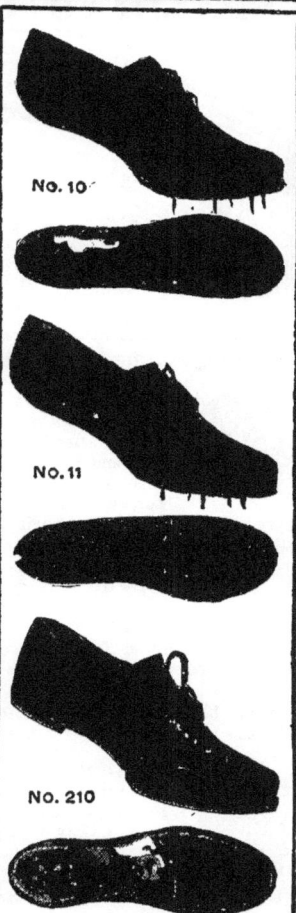

Spalding Running Shoes

No. 2-0. This Running Shoe is made of the finest Kangaroo leather; extremely light and glove fitting. Best English steel spikes firmly riveted on. Per pair, **$6.00**

No. 10. Finest Calfskin Running Shoe; light weight, hand made, six spikes. Per pair, **$5.00**

No. 11T. Calfskin, machine made, solid leather tap sole holds spikes firmly in place. Per pair, **$4.00**

No. 11. Calfskin, machine made. Per pair, **$3.00**

Juvenile Running Shoes

No. 12. Outdoor Leather Running Shoes, complete with spikes, in sizes 12 to 5 only. Per pair, **$2.50**

No. 115. Indoor Leather Running Shoes, without spikes, in boys' sizes, 12 to 5 inclusive, only Pair. **$2.00**

Indoor Running Shoes
With or Without Spikes

No. 111. Fine leather, rubber tipped sole, with spikes. Per pair, **$4.00**

No. 112. Leather shoe, special corrugated rubber tap sole, no spikes. **$3.00**

No. 114. Leather shoe, rubber tipped, no spikes. **$2.50**

Indoor Jumping Shoes
With or Without Spikes

No. 210. Hand made, best leather, rubber soles. **$5.00**

Protection for Running Shoe Spikes

No. N. Thick wood, shaped and perforated to accomodate spikes. Per pair **50c**

Spalding Special Grips With Elastic No. 2. Best quality cork with elastic bands. Pair. **20c.**

No. 1. **Athletic Grips** Selected cork, shaped to fit hollow of hand. Pair. **15c.**

Chamois Pushers No. 5. Fine chamois skin and used with running, walking, jumping and other athletic shoes. Pair, **25c.**

| PROMPT ATTENTION GIVEN TO ANY COMMUNICATIONS ADDRESSED TO US | **A. G. SPALDING & BROS.** STORES IN ALL LARGE CITIES | FOR COMPLETE LIST OF STORES SEE INSIDE FRONT COVER OF THIS BOOK |

Prices in effect January 5, 1910. Subject to change without notice. For Canadian prices see special Canadian Catalogue.

SPALDING CHAMPIONSHIP HAMMER
With Ball Bearing Swivel

JOHN FLANAGAN
16-lb Hammer Thrower

The Spalding Championship Ball Bearing Hammer, originally designed by John Flanagan, has been highly endorsed only after repeated trials in championship events. The benefits of the ball bearing construction will be quickly appreciated by all hammer throwers. Guaranteed absolutely correct in weight.

No. 12FB. 12-lb., with sole leather case. $7.50
No. 12F. 12-lb., without sole leather case. 5.50
No. 16FB. 16-lb., with sole leather case. 7.50
No. 16F. 16-lb., without sole leather case. 5.50

Spalding Rubber Covered Indoor Shot
Patented December 19, 1905

This shot is made according to scientific principles, with a rubber cover that is perfectly round; gives a fine grip, and has the proper resiliency when it comes in contact with the floor; will wear longer than the ordinary leather covered, and in addition there is no possibility that the lead dust will sift out, therefore it is always full weight.
No. P. 16-lb. $10.00 | No. Q. 12-lb. $9.00

Spalding Indoor Shot
With our improved leather cover. Does not lose weight even when used constantly.
No. 3. 12-lb. Each, $7.00
No. 4. 16-lb. " 7.50

Regulation Shot, Lead and Iron
Guaranteed Correct in Weight

No. 16LS. 16-lb., lead. Each, $3.50
No. 12LS. 12-lb., lead. 3.00
No. 16IS. 16-lb., iron. 1.75
No. 12IS. 12-lb., iron. 1.50

Spalding Regulation Hammer
With Wire Handle
Guaranteed Correct in Weight
Lead
No. 12LH. 12-lb., lead, practice $4.50
No. 16LH. 16-lb., lead, regulation. 5.00
Iron
No. 12IH. 12-lb., iron, practice. 3.50
No. 16IH. 16-lb., iron, regulation. 3.75

Extra Wire Handles
No. FH. For above hammers, improved design, large grip, heavy wire. Each, 75c.

Spalding Regulation 56-lb. Weight

Made after model submitted by Champion J. S. Mitchel, and endorsed by all weight throwers. Packed in box and guaranteed correct in weight and in exact accordance with rules of A. A. U.
No. 2. Lead 56-lb. weights Complete, $12.00

SPALDING JUVENILE ATHLETIC SHOT AND HAMMERS
Spalding Juvenile Athletic Shot and Hammers are made according to official regulations. Weights are guaranteed accurate and records made with these implements will be recognized.

JUVENILE HAMMER
No. 8IH. 8-lb., Iron, Juvenile Hammer. Each, $2.50
JUVENILE SHOT
No. 26. 8-lb., Leather Covered Shot, for indoor, schoolyard and playground use. Each, $5.00
No. 5. 5-lb., Leather Covered Shot, for indoor, schoolyard and playground use. " 3.00
No. 8IS. 8-lb., Solid Iron Shot, not covered. Each, $1.25
No. 5IS. 5-lb., Solid Iron Shot, not covered. " 1.00

ACCEPT NO SUBSTITUTE — **THE SPALDING TRADE-MARK** — **GUARANTEES QUALITY**

Spalding Olympic Discus

Since the introduction of Discus Throwing, which was revived at the Olympic Games, at Athens, in 1896, and which was one of the principal features at the recent games held there, the Spalding Discus has been recognized as the official Discus, and is used in all competitions because it conforms exactly to the official rules in every respect, and is exactly the same as used at Athens, 1906, and London, 1908. Packed in sealed box, and guaranteed absolutely correct. . . . . Price, **$5.00**

Spalding Youths' Discus

Officially adopted by the Public Schools Athletic League. To satisfy the demand for a Discus that will be suitable for the use of the more youthful athletes, we have put out a special Discus smaller in size and lighter in weight than the regular Official size. The Youths' Discus is made in accordance with official specifications. Price, **$4.00**

Spalding Vaulting Standards

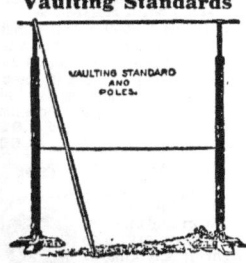

These Standards are made carefully and well. There is nothing flimsy about them, and the measurements are clearly and correctly marked, so as to avoid any misunderstanding or dispute.
No. **109.** Wooden uprights, graduated in half-inches, adjustable to 13 feet.
Complete, **$15.00**
No. **111.** Wooden uprights, inch graduations, 7 feet high. Complete, **$9.00**
No. **112. Cross Bars.** Hickory. Dozen, **$3.00**

Spalding Official Javelins

No. **53.** Swedish model, correct in length, weight, etc., and of proper balance. Steel shod. . . . . Each, **$3.50**

Spalding Vaulting Poles—Selected Spruce, Solid

The greatest care has been exercised in making these poles. In selecting the spruce only the most perfect and thoroughly seasoned pieces have been used. All of this goes to make them what we claim they are, the only poles really fit and safe for an athlete to use.
No. **103.** 14 feet long. . . . . . Each, **$6.00**
No. **104.** 16 feet long. . . . . . " **7.00**

We guarantee all of our wood vaulting poles to be perfect in material and workmanship, but we do *not* guarantee against breaks while in use, as we have found in our experience that they are usually caused by improper use or abuse.

Spalding Bamboo Vaulting Poles

Tape wound at short intervals. Thoroughly tested before leaving our factory. Fitted with special spike.
No. **10BV.** 10 feet long. . . . . . Each, **$4.00**
No. **12BV.** 12 feet long. . . . . . " **4.50**
No. **14BV.** 14 feet long. . . . . . " **5.00**
No. **16BV.** 16 feet long. . . . . . " **5.00**

Competitors' Numbers

Printed on Heavy Manila Paper or Strong Linen

No.	MANILA Per Set	LINEN Per Set
No. 1. 1 to 50.	$ .25	$1.50
No. 2. 1 to 75.	.38	2.25
No. 3. 1 to 100.	.50	3.00
No. 4. 1 to 150.	.75	4.50
No. 5. 1 to 200.	1.00	6.00
No. 6. 1 to 250.	1.25	7.50

For larger meets we supply Competitors' Numbers on Manila paper only in sets as follows:

No.	PER SET	No.	PER SET
7. 1 to 300.	$1.50	16. 1 to 1200.	$6.00
8. 1 to 400.	2.00	17. 1 to 1300.	6.50
9. 1 to 500.	2.50	18. 1 to 1400.	7.00
10. 1 to 600.	3.00	19. 1 to 1500.	7.50
11. 1 to 700.	3.50	20. 1 to 1600.	8.00
12. 1 to 800.	4.00	21. 1 to 1700.	8.50
13. 1 to 900.	4.50	22. 1 to 1800.	9.00
14. 1 to 1000.	5.00	23. 1 to 1900.	9.50
15. 1 to 1100.	5.50	24. 1 to 2000.	10.00

PROMPT ATTENTION GIVEN TO ANY COMMUNICATIONS ADDRESSED TO US — **A. G. SPALDING & BROS.** STORES IN ALL LARGE CITIES — FOR COMPLETE LIST OF STORES SEE INSIDE FRONT COVER OF THIS BOOK

Prices in effect January 5, 1910. Subject to change without notice. For Canadian prices see special Canadian Catalogue.

ACCEPT NO SUBSTITUTE THE SPALDING TRADE-MARK GUARANTEES QUALITY

Spalding Athletic Paraphernalia

Foster's Patent Safety Hurdle
The frame is 2 feet 6 inches high, with a swinging wooden hurdle 2 feet high, the swinging joint being 6 inches from one side and 18 inches from the other. With the short side up it measures 2 feet 6 inches from the ground, and with the long side up, 3 feet 6 inches. The hurdle can be changed from one height to the other in a few seconds, and is held firmly in either position by a thumb-screw.
Single Hurdle, **$3.50**

Foster's Safety Hurdle at the World's Fair, St. Louis

Spalding 7-Foot Circle

The discus, shot and weights are thrown from the 7-foot circle. Made of one piece band iron with bolted joints. Circle painted white. Each, **$10.00**

Spalding Take-off Board
The Take-off Board is used for the running broad jump, and is a necessary adjunct to the athletic field. Regulation size; top painted white. Each, **$3.00**

Spalding Toe Board or Stop Board
The Toe Board or Stop Board is used when putting the 16-lb. shot, throwing weights and discus, and is curved on the arc of a 7-foot circle. Toe Board, regulation size, painted white and substantially made. Each, **$3.50**

Spalding Referees' Whistles
No. **1.** Nickel-plated whistle, well made. Each, **25c.**
No. **2.** Very reliable. Popular design. Each, **25c.**

Spalding Lanes for Sprint Races
We supply in this set sufficient stakes and cord to lay out four 100-yard lanes. Stakes are made with pointed end and sufficiently strong, so that they can be driven into hard ground.
No. **L.** Per set, **$15.00**

Patent Steel Tape Chain on Patent Electric Reel
For Measuring Distances in Athletic Competitions
Made of superior steel about ¼ inch wide. The reel allows the entire tape open to dry and can be reeled and unreeled as easily as tapes in cases. Especially adapted to lay off courses and long measurements.
No. **1B.** 100 feet long. Each, **$5.00**
No. **11B.** 200 feet long. " **7.50**

Patent "Angle" Steel Measuring Tape
Especially adapted for laying off base ball diamonds, tennis courts and all kinds of athletic fields, both outdoors and indoors. Right angles accurately determined; also equally good for straight or any kind of measuring. Enclosed in hard leather case, flush handles. All mountings nickel-plated.
No. **A.** 50 feet long, ⅜ inch wide. Each, **$4.00**
No. **B.** 100 feet long, ⅜ inch wide. " **6.75**

Spalding Stop Watch
Stem winder, nickel-plated case, porcelain dial, registered to 60 seconds by 1-5 seconds, fly back engaging and disengaging mechanism. Each, **$7.50**

Spalding Starter's Pistol
32 caliber, two inch barrel, patent ejecting device. Each, **$6.00**

Spalding Official Sacks for Sack Races
(REINFORCED)

Spalding Official Sacks for Sack Races are made in two sizes, for men and boys. They are all strongly reinforced, will wear for a great length of time, and by their construction it is practically impossible for racers to work their feet free. These sacks are made in exact accordance with official regulations.
No. **MS.** Men's Sack, reinforced, 3 ft. wide. Ea., **$1.50**
No. **BS.** Boys' Sack, reinforced, 2½ ft. wide. Ea., **$1.00**

Official Harness for Three-Legged Racing
Made according to official rules. Complete set of straps for fastening men and with extra straps for keeping fastenings at required height in long distances races.

No. **1.** Official Harness for Three-Legged Racing. Per set, **$2.50**

| PROMPT ATTENTION GIVEN TO ANY COMMUNICATIONS ADDRESSED TO US | **A. G. SPALDING & BROS.**
STORES IN ALL LARGE CITIES | FOR COMPLETE LIST OF STORES SEE INSIDE FRONT COVER OF THIS BOOK |

Prices in effect January 5, 1910. Subject to change without notice. For Canadian prices see special Canadian Catalogue.

ACCEPT NO SUBSTITUTE — **THE SPALDING** — **TRADE-MARK** — **GUARANTEES QUALITY**

The Spalding Official Basket Ball

THE ONLY OFFICIAL BASKET BALL

WE GUARANTEE this ball to be perfect in material and workmanship and correct in shape and size when inspected at our factory. If any defect is discovered during the first game in which it is used, or during the first day's practice use, and, if returned at once, we will replace same under this guarantee. We do not guarantee against ordinary wear nor against defect in shape or size that is not discovered immediately after the first day's use.

Owing to the superb quality of our No. M Basket Ball, our customers have grown to expect a season's use of one ball, and at times make unreasonable claims under our guarantee, which we will not allow.

A. G. SPALDING & BROS.

OFFICIALLY ADOPTED AND STANDARD. The cover is made in four sections, with capless ends, and of the finest and most carefully selected pebble grain English leather. We take the entire output of this superior grade of leather from the English tanners, and in the Official Basket Ball use the choicest parts of each hide. The bladder is made especially for this ball of extra quality pure Para rubber (no composition.) Each ball packed complete, in sealed box, with rawhide lace and lacing needle, and guaranteed perfect in every detail. To provide that all official contests may be held under absolutely fair and uniform conditions, it is stipulated that this ball must be used in all match games of either men's or women's teams.

No. M. Spalding "Official" Basket Ball. Each, $6.00

Extract from Men's Official Rule Book
RULE II—BALL.
SEC. 3. The ball made by A.G. Spalding & Bros. shall be the official ball. Official balls will be stamped as herewith, and will be in sealed boxes.
SEC. 4. The official ball must be used in all match games.

Extract from Official Collegiate Rule Book
The Spalding Official Basket Ball No. M is the official ball of the Intercollegiate Basket Ball Association, and must be used in all match games.

Extract from Women's Official Rule Book
RULE II—BALL.
SEC. 3. The ball made by A.G. Spalding & Bros. shall be the official ball. Official balls will be stamped as herewith, and will be in sealed boxes.
SEC. 4. The official ball must be used in all match games.

PROMPT ATTENTION GIVEN TO ANY COMMUNICATIONS ADDRESSED TO US — **A. G. SPALDING & BROS.** STORES IN ALL LARGE CITIES — FOR COMPLETE LIST OF STORES SEE INSIDE FRONT COVER OF THIS BOOK

Prices in effect January 5, 1910. Subject to change without notice. For Canadian prices see special Canadian Catalogue.

ACCEPT NO SUBSTITUTE — **THE SPALDING TRADE-MARK** — **GUARANTEES QUALITY**

Spalding "Special No. E"

No. E. Fine pebble grain leather case. The bladder of pure Para rubber (no composition) and guaranteed. Each ball complete in sealed box, with rawhide lace and lacing needle.
Each, **$4.50**

Spalding "Official" Basket Ball Goals

Officially adopted and must be used in all match games. We are equipping our basket ball goals now with nets constructed so that the bottom may be left open in practice games to permit ball to drop through. The opening is closed readily by a draw string for match games.
No. **80.** Per pair, **$4.00**

Extract from Official Rule Book
RULE III.—GOALS
SEC. 3. The goal made by A. G. SPALDING & BROS. shall be the official goal.
SEC. 4. The official goal must be used in all match games.

Spalding Detachable Basket Ball Goals

No. **50.** Made so that they may be detached readily from the wall or upright, leaving no obstruction to interfere with other games or with general gymnasium work. Same size basket and brace, same length as on official goals. Per pair, **$5.00**

Pat. May 25, 1909 **Spalding Practice Goals**
No. **70.** Japanned Iron Rings and Brackets. Complete with nets. Per pair, **$3.00**

Spalding Outdoor Goals

Spalding Practice "No. 18"

No. **18.** Good quality leather cover. Each ball complete in box with pure Para rubber (no composition) bladder guaranteed; rawhide lace and lacing needle. Each, **$3.00**
No. **O1.** Canvas Cover, for holding inflated basket ball.
Each, **$1.00**

The upright post is made of 4x6 inch selected chestnut. The backstop itself is made of tongue and groove chestnut, all of the woodwork being given two coats of durable outdoor paint. Furnished complete with pair of No. 80 Official Basket Ball Goals.
No. **160.** Pair, **$40.00**

Spalding Backstops Only for Basket Ball Goals

These backstops are made of ⅞-inch matched hard wood. The back of the board is reinforced by three cleats of 2 x 2⅝ inch material. On flat walls the two end cleats extend above and below the backstop, which is attached to the wall by bolting through these cleats.
No. **100.** Per pair, **$20.00**

Spalding Thumb Protector

No. **T.** A substantial support that players will appreciate.
Each, **50c.**

Spalding Basket Ball Score Books

No. **1.** Paper cover, 10 games, **10c.**
No. **2.** Cloth cover, 25 games, **25c.**
No. **A.** Collegiate, paper cover, 10 games. Each, **10c.**
No. **B.** Collegiate, cloth cover, 25 games. Each, **25c.**

Spalding Bladders—Guaranteed Quality

All rubber bladders bearing our Trade-Mark are made of pure Para rubber (no composition), and are guaranteed perfect in material and workmanship. Note special explanation of guarantee on tag attached to each bladder.
No. **OM.** For No. M ball. . . . Each, **$1.50**
No. **16.** For No. E ball. . . . " **1.00**
No. **A.** For No. 18 ball. . . . " **1.00**

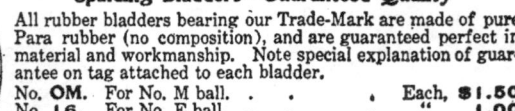

PROMPT ATTENTION GIVEN TO ANY COMMUNICATIONS ADDRESSED TO US | **A. G. SPALDING & BROS.** STORES IN ALL LARGE CITIES | FOR COMPLETE LIST OF STORES SEE INSIDE FRONT COVER OF THIS BOOK

Prices in effect January 5, 1910. Subject to change without notice. For Canadian prices see special Canadian Catalogue.

SPALDING BASKET BALL SHOES

Spalding Basket Ball Shoes, on account of their general satisfactory qualities, are worn by the most prominent teams and fastest players in the country.

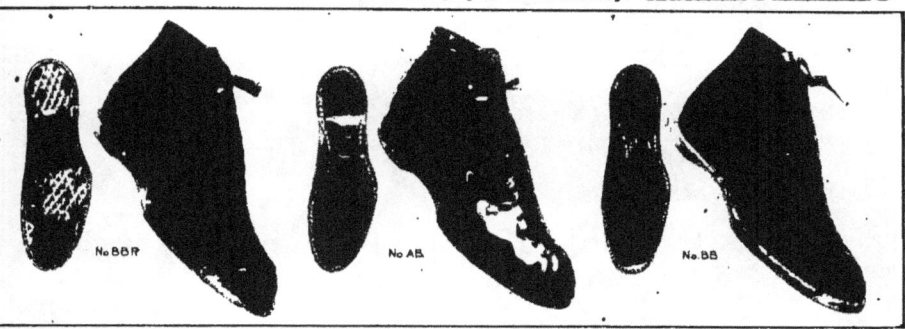

No. BBR. THE SPALDING "EXPERT" BASKET BALL SHOES. Pure gum thick rubber soles, with special diamond point surface and reinforced edges to prevent sole spreading. Laces extremely far down. Made of best quality black calf in highest type of workmanship. The soles on these shoes are perfectly made but we do not guarantee as to length of service. . Pair, **$10.00**

No. AB. SPALDING BASKET BALL SHOES. The red rubber suction soles we use on these shoes are superior quality and 1-16 inch thicker than the soles on the No. BB shoes. One of the principal advantages of this style of sole is that it enables the player to obtain a good, firm purchase on the floor. Superior quality light drab chrome tan leather. Laces extremely far down. Pair, **$5.00**

No. BB. SPALDING BASKET BALL SHOES. Suction soles of good quality red rubber. Uppers of good quality black leather. A very popular style of basket ball shoe. Per pair, **$3.50**

No. BBL. SPALDING BASKET BALL SHOES FOR LADIES. These are otherwise same as No. BB shoe. . Pair, **$3.50**

SPALDING CANVAS TOP BASKET BALL SHOES

No. HH. High cut white canvas upper. Sole surface is similar to our popular gymnasium shoes, but of white, best quality rubber, twice as thick as on best rubber sole gymnasium shoe. A very durable and satisfactory shoe. Sizes 6 to 12 inclusive. Per pair, **$2.00**
No. HHB. Boys' sizes, 2½ to 5½ inclusive. Otherwise same as HH. Pair, **$1.85**

SPALDING JUVENILE BASKET BALL SHOES
No. BBX. A Boy's Basket Ball Shoe made on special boys' size lasts. Material of good quality and general construction similar to our regular line of men's shoes. Sole similar to No. BB shoe. Furnished in boys' sizes 12 to 5 inclusive, only. . . Pair, **$2.50**

No. HHX. Youths' sizes, 11 to 2 inc. Otherwise same as HH. Pr. **1.70**
No. H. Same as No. HH, but low cut. Sizes 6 to 12 inc. " **1.75**
No. HB. Boys' sizes, 2½ to 5½ inc, Otherwise same as No. H. " **1.60**
No. HX. Youths' sizes, 11 to 2 inc. Otherwise same as No. H. " **1.45**

Spalding Special Basket Ball Pants

No. 6B. Good quality, either Gray or White flannel, padded lightly on hips; very loose fitting. Pair, **$1.75**
No. 5B. Heavy Brown or White canvas, padded lightly on hips; very loose fitting. Pair, **$1.00**
No. 7B. White silesia, hips lightly padded; very loose fitting. Pair, **75c.**
No. 40P. Padded knee length pants. White silesia. Pair, **$1.00**
No. 40. Similar to No. 40P, but unpadded. . . " **.75**

No. 40P   No. 5B

A. G. SPALDING & BROS.
STORES IN ALL LARGE CITIES

PROMPT ATTENTION GIVEN TO ANY COMMUNICATIONS ADDRESSED TO US

FOR COMPLETE LIST OF STORES SEE INSIDE FRONT COVER OF THIS BOOK

Prices in effect January 5, 1910. Subject to change without notice. For Canadian prices see special Canadian Catalogue.

ACCEPT NO SUBSTITUTE THE SPALDING TRADE-MARK **GUARANTEES QUALITY**

Spalding All-Steel Playground Apparatus

Acknowledged as the Standard. Specified and purchased by practically all Municipal Park and Playground Commissions in America.

SPALDING PLAYGROUND APPARATUS IS USED IN

Alameda, Cal.	Dayton, O.	Kentfield, Cal.	Naugatuck, Ct.	Pittsburg, Pa.	Somerville, Mass.
Allegheny, Pa.	Denver, Col.	Lancaster, Pa.	Newark, N. J.	Pocatello, Idaho	St. Louis, Mo
Ashburnham, Mass.	Dongan Hills, N. Y.	Leavenworth, Kan.	New Brunswick, N. J.	Polk, Pa.	Summit, N. J.
Baltimore, Md.	East Orange, N. J.	Lexington, Ind.	New Haven, Ct.	Portland, Me.	Utica, N. Y.
Bayonne, N. J.	Forest Park, Md.	Lockhart, Ala.	New London, Ct.	Portland, Ore.	Walla Walla, Wash.
Bloomfield, N. J.	Ft. Plain, N. Y.	Los Angeles, Cal.	New Paltz, N. Y.	Porto Barrios, S. Am.	Washington, D. C.
Boston, Mass.	Ft. Wayne, Ind.	Louisville, Ky.	New York, N. Y.	Pueblo, Col.	Watertown, Mass.
Brooklyn, N. Y.	Galesburg, Ill.	Lowell, Mass.	Oakland, Cal.	Reading, Pa.	Watervliet, N. Y.
Bryn Mawr, Pa.	Geneva, N. Y.	Lynn, Mass.	Omaha, Neb.	Rochester, N. Y.	Westfield, Mass.
Buffalo, N. Y.	Greeley, Col.	Madison, N. J.	Orange, N. J.	Rye, N. Y.	Wilkesbarre, Pa.
Catskill, N. Y.	Hamilton, Ontario, Can.	Melrose, Mass.	Oswego, N. Y.	Sag Harbor, N. Y.	Winnipeg, Man., Can.
Chicago, Ill.	Havana, Cuba	Meridian, Miss.	Pasadena, Cal.	San Jose, Cal.	Winthrop, Mass.
Cincinnati, O.	Hoboken, N. J.	Milwaukee, Wis.	Passaic, N. J.	Seattle, Wash.	Worcester, Mass.
Cleveland, O.	Jersey City, N. J.	Morristown, N. J.	Philadelphia, Pa.	Springfield, Mass.	Ypsilanti, Mich.
Dallas, Texas	Kansas City, Mo.	Nashville, Tenn.			

Correspondence Invited.   Special Plans and Estimates on Request.

A. G. SPALDING & BROS., Inc.
Gymnasium and Playground Contract Department
CHICOPEE, MASS.

| PROMPT ATTENTION GIVEN TO ANY COMMUNICATIONS ADDRESSED TO US | A. G. SPALDING & BROS. STORES IN ALL LARGE CITIES | FOR COMPLETE LIST OF STORES SEE INSIDE FRONT COVER OF THIS BOOK |

Prices in effect January 5, 1910. Subject to change without notice. For Canadian prices see special Canadian Catalogue.

ACCEPT NO SUBSTITUTE — THE SPALDING TRADE-MARK GUARANTEES QUALITY

THE SPALDING TRADE-MARK IS PLACED UPON EVERY GENUINE SPALDING ARTICLE. ACCEPT NO SUBSTITUTE.

Spalding Home Gymnasium
Combining Swinging Rings, Trapeze, Stirrups and Swing

Can be put up Anywhere

Especially adapted for use by Boys and Girls

HOME APPARATUS

Start with the boy by making him take some kind of exercise, and if he is not inclined to do so without urging, provide him with suitable apparatus that is at the same time interesting. It won't be long before you will see the effects in his improved physique and no urging will be necessary to induce him to show off his prowess on swinging rings or trapeze. The boy that is started this way grows up with the inclination for athletic exercises that will keep him in good health during the balance of his life.

The apparatus is supported by two strong screw-hooks in the ceiling, about eighteen inches apart. It can also be used out of doors. The straps are of extra strong webbing and adjustable to any desired height; rings heavily japanned. The apparatus can be put up in any room, and removed in a moment, leaving only two hooks in the ceiling visible. The various combinations can be quickly and easily made. We furnish in addition, a board, adjustable to the stirrups which forms an excellent swing.

No. 1. Complete, ready to put up, **$6.00**

No. 201. Adjustable Trapeze

No. 301. Adjustable Swinging Rings

Spalding Adjustable Trapeze and Swinging Rings

Furnished complete, with everything necessary for suspending. The supports are made of extra strong webbing. Perfectly safe under all conditions and with the adjustable buckle may be adapted to any ceiling from 16 feet down.

No. 201. Trapeze. . **$3.50**
No. 301. Complete with 6-inch Japanned Swinging Rings. **$3.50**

PROMPT ATTENTION GIVEN TO ANY COMMUNICATIONS ADDRESSED TO US
A. G. SPALDING & BROS.
STORES IN ALL LARGE CITIES
FOR COMPLETE LIST OF STORES SEE INSIDE FRONT COVER OF THIS BOOK

Prices in effect January 5, 1910. Subject to change without notice. For Canadian prices see special Canadian Catalogue.

ACCEPT NO SUBSTITUTE THE SPALDING TRADE-MARK **GUARANTEES QUALITY**

THE SPALDING TRADE-MARK IS PLACED UPON EVERY GENUINE SPALDING ARTICLE. ACCEPT NO SUBSTITUTE.

Spalding Chest Weight

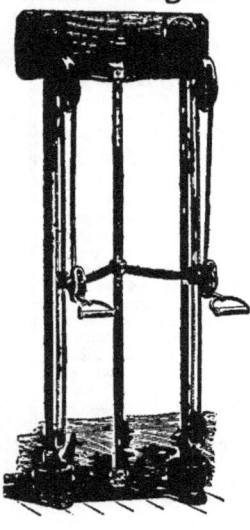

This machine has the Center Arm Adjustment, which permits of all the lower as well as the direct and upper chest movements. The various changes are made by raising or lowering the center arm, requiring but a few seconds. It really combines two machines in one, and is particularly suitable for home use where space is a consideration. Japan finish. One of the most reliable and satisfactory machines ever built. Each Machine is equipped with 16 pounds of weights.

**CHEST WEIGHT MACHINE
No. 5. . Each, $15.00**

Spalding Foot and Leg Attachment

Illustrating Method of Fastening Foot and Leg Attachment to No. 5 Chest Weight Machine.

No. 2. Well made of heavy cowhide. Readily attached to one handle or both; can be worn with or without shoe. Each, $1.50

Spalding Head and Neck Attachment

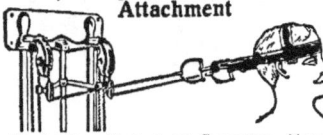

Illustrating Method of Fastening Head and Neck Attachment to No. 5 Chest Weight Machine.

No. 3. Well made of heavy cowhide, Ready for use by simply snapping to one of the handles or both. Each, $1.50

Spalding Rowing Attachments

The Rowing Attachments listed below, which are to be used in connection with Chest Weight Machines, will be found particularly suitable for home use, as they may be detached from the weight machine quickly and can then be put away in a very small space until the next opportunity for use presents itself.

To be used in connection only with chest weights which have center arm adjustment, or with handles arranged so that they can be pulled from a bracket close to the floor.

No. 1. This attachment as will be noted, has out-riggers and arms similar to the rowing machine, and offers a great variety of work when used in connection with the chest weight. . . . . Complete, $10.00

No. 2. Designed to fill the demand for a low priced article of this kind, built along substantial lines. Will give entire satisfaction. . Complete, $8.00

NOTE—These Attachments can be used only in connection with the No. 5 Type of Chest Weight Machine.

Home Apparatus

Home apparatus, suitable for home use, and not altogether by the boys and girls of the household, but by the grownups; as a matter of fact, the ones who usually require exercise of a rational kind much more than the younger generation who have the time and inclination for outdoor exercise not possessed by many of their elders—that is what we will attempt to show in this section of our catalogue.

Used in connection with our various Athletic Libraries there is no reason why any man cannot practically renew his youthful vigor.

PROMPT ATTENTION GIVEN TO ANY COMMUNICATIONS ADDRESSED TO US **A. G. SPALDING & BROS.** STORES IN ALL LARGE CITIES FOR COMPLETE LIST OF STORES SEE INSIDE FRONT COVER OF THIS BOOK

Prices in effect January 5, 1910. Subject to change without notice. For Canadian prices see special Canadian Catalogue.

Spalding Home Apparatus

Exercise acts on the health of an individual in the same way as the draught does on the fire in a furnace. Pile on the coal and shut off the draught and you kill the fire. Continue to eat heavy meals and take no exercise and your health will be affected, not because of the food you have eaten so much as on account of the lack of exercise. A little exercise is all that is necessary to keep you in good condition. Some rational, pleasant and interesting exercise, persisted in with regularity and, preferably, with Spalding Home Apparatus, will help you to retain your health.

Spalding Chest Weight No. 2

An ideal machine for home use. Well made and easy running. Rods are ⅜-inch coppered spring steel. Bearings are hardened steel cone points running in soft, gray iron, noiseless and durable. Weight carriage packed with felt, good for long wear, but easily removed and replaced when necessary without the use of glue or wedges of any kind. Weight carriage strikes on rubber bumpers. Weights are 5-pound iron dumb-bells, one to each carriage, and may be removed and used as dumb bells. Wall and floor boards are hard wood, nicely finished and stained. All castings heavily japanned. Every part of machine guaranteed free of defect.
No. 2.   Each, $5.00

Spalding Chest Weight No. 12

We have just added this very well made machine to our line. Cast iron parts are all nicely japanned. The wheels are iron, turned true on centers, and have hardened steel cone point bearings. The guide rods are spring steel, copper-plated. The weight carriage has removable felt bushings, noiseless and durable. Each handle is equipped with 10 lbs. of weights.
No. 12. - Each, $10.00

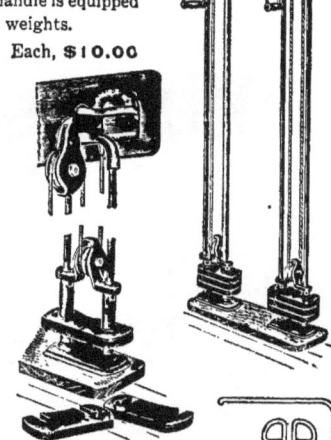

Showing important details of Construction of No. 12 Machine.

PROMPT ATTENTION GIVEN TO ANY COMMUNICATIONS ADDRESSED TO US

A. G. SPALDING & BROS.
STORES IN ALL LARGE CITIES

FOR COMPLETE LIST OF STORES SEE INSIDE FRONT COVER OF THIS BOOK

Prices in effect January 5, 1910. Subject to change without notice. For Canadian prices see special Canadian Catalogue.

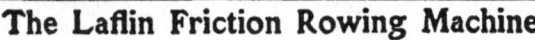

THE SPALDING TRADE-MARK IS PLACED UPON EVERY GENUINE SPALDING ARTICLE. ACCEPT NO SUBSTITUTE.

The Laflin Friction Rowing Machine

Do not use oil on friction cylinder. If its action is not perfectly smooth a little clear soap rubbed on its surface will properly correct its action. The means used to produce the resistance is a simple friction clutch, which takes instant hold at the commencement of the stroke and retains the pressure till its completion, when it instantly releases it precisely as in a boat. Quickly taken apart without loosening any bolts or screws. Each machine is adjustable to any amount of friction or resistance.

No. 119. Complete, $16.00

Home Apparatus

The apparatus listed in this catalogue is designed particularly for private use; i. e., in homes and private gymnasiums. It retains the same superior marks of quality which distinguish the regular line of gymnasium apparatus manufactured by A. G. Spalding & Bros., but its distinctive design permits it to be sold at a price more in keeping with its use than heretofore obtainable, without any sacrifice of practical value or durability.

Kerns' Rowing Machine

Operated just like rowing a boat

Suitable alike for the Athlete or the ordinary Man or Woman

The ideal boat for home use and training purposes. Used by the leading athletic clubs, colleges and prominent oarsmen of the world, and pronounced the most perfect rowing machine ever produced. Fitted with the Kerns' Patent Roller Seat and Shoes, the shoes having a three-inch adjustment, to suit either a tall or a short person. By turning a thumb-nut the belt can be tightened to any desired degree, and more or less friction thrown into the running parts, imitating the resistance which exists when forcing a row-boat through the water. The weaker sex can use the machine by simply loosening the thumb-nut which reduces the resistance; and on the other hand, by reversing the operation the resistance can be so increased that the strongest athlete can have any amount of resistance. The oars are pivoted in such a way that the operator can handle and turn them the same as he would during the return and feathering motion with a boat oar.

No. 600. Kerns' Patent Single Scull Rowing Machine. . . . Each, $30.00

| PROMPT ATTENTION GIVEN TO ANY COMMUNICATIONS ADDRESSED TO US | **A. G. SPALDING & BROS.** STORES IN ALL LARGE CITIES | FOR COMPLETE LIST OF STORES SEE INSIDE FRONT COVER OF THIS BOOK |

Prices in effect January 5, 1910. Subject to change without notice. For Canadian prices see special Canadian Catalogue.

The Spalding Championship Gloves

The Spalding "Championship" Gloves are endorsed by all champions and have been exclusively used for years in championship contests and in training. The material and workmanship are of the highest quality, the fit is perfect, and by their peculiar construction absolutely prevent any chance of injury to the hands or wrists. Each set is carefully inspected before packing and guaranteed in every particular. Made in three sizes in sets of four gloves.

Used and Endorsed by Champions of the World

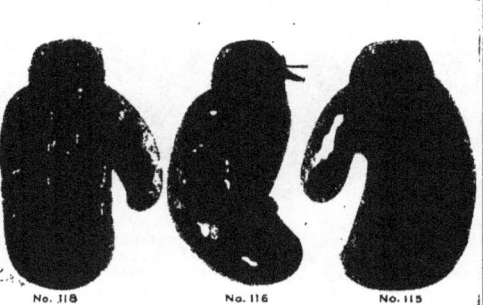

No. 118. No. 116. No. 115.

No. 115. The Spalding 5-oz. "Championship" Glove. Per set of four gloves, **$6.00**

No. 116. The Spalding 6-oz. "Championship" Glove. Per set of four gloves, **$6.00**

No. 118. The Spalding 8-oz. "Championship" Glove. Per set of four gloves, **$6.50**

Spalding "Special" No. 218
Same style as our "Championship" 8-oz. Gloves, but not same quality material and workmanship. No. 218. Per set of four gloves, **$4.50**

BURNS vs. JOHNSON
SPALDING GLOVES USED
Kerry Copyright.

Spalding "Navy Special" Championship Gloves
Used by the Champions of the Navy
These gloves are made of a special "sea green" leather, of particularly durable quality. Furnished in 8-oz. only, similar in style to No. 118, and with padded wrist. No. 18N. Per set of four gloves, **$5.00**

BOXING IN THE NAVY
COPYRIGHT, 1905, BY G. W. FAWCETT

Spalding Pupil's Boxing Gloves
Acting on the suggestion of one of the most prominent athletic officials in this country, we decided recently to get up a boxing glove that would be an aid to the pupil learning to box. This glove is additionally padded on the forearm and over the wrist, to prevent that soreness which is one of the most discouraging features following a brisk lesson in the art of "blocking."

Spalding Pupil's Boxing Glove
Padding on Wrist and Forearm.
The glove part is well padded with curled hair, the leather being best quality soft tanned. No. 110. Per set of four gloves, **$6.00**

The Spalding Instructors' Gloves, 10-oz.
Made of best grade brown glove leather, extra heavily padded over the knuckles and with special large padded thumb to prevent injury to either instructor or pupil. Laces extra far to provide ample ventilation and has patent palm grip.
No. 100. Per set of four gloves, **$6.00**

The Spalding 5-oz. Boxing Gloves
None Better at Any Price
Made of special quality light tan-colored glove leather, very soft and smooth. Plain laced wrist-band, patent palm lacing and patent palm grip. An ideal glove for limited round contests.
No. 105. Per set of four gloves, **$7.00**

EACH SET OF BOXING GLOVES CONSISTS OF FOUR GLOVES, MATED IN TWO PAIRS

PROMPT ATTENTION GIVEN TO ANY COMMUNICATIONS ADDRESSED TO US | **A. G. SPALDING & BROS.** STORES IN ALL LARGE CITIES | FOR COMPLETE LIST OF STORES SEE INSIDE FRONT COVER OF THIS BOOK

Prices in effect January 5, 1910. Subject to change without notice - For Canadian prices see special Canadian Catalogue.

Spalding Boxing Gloves

ACCEPT NO SUBSTITUTE — THE SPALDING TRADE-MARK **GUARANTEES QUALITY**

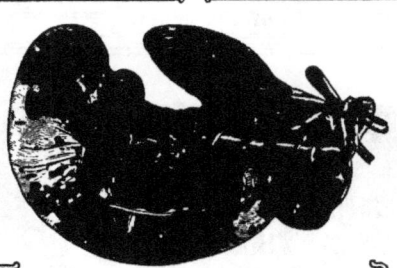

No. 11. Corbett pattern, large 7-oz. glove, best quality brown glove leather, padded with best curled hair, patent palm lacing, padded wristband, patent palm grip. Substantially made throughout for hard usage.
Set of four gloves, **$5.00**

No. 9. Regulation 5-oz. glove, otherwise same as No. 11.
Set of four gloves, **$5.00**

No. 14. Regulation 5-oz. glove, dark wine color, padded wristband, patent palm lacing and palm grip. Much improved.
Set of four gloves, **$4.00**

No. 15. Corbett pattern; olive tanned leather, well padded with hair, padded wristband, patent palm lacing, patent palm grip.
Set of four gloves, **$4.00**

No. 17. Corbett pattern, craven tan leather, well padded with hair, patent palm lacing, patent palm grip, padded wristband.
Set of four gloves, **$4.00**

Above illustrates the patent palm lacing and patent palm grip referred to in descriptions of Spalding boxing gloves. With these improvements we believe our line is absolutely the finest on the market. The patent palm lacing, insuring a snug fit at all times, is a very valuable feature, and the patent palm grip we know, will be appreciated by those who want gloves that are up-to-date in every particular.

No. 11. Corbett Pattern

No. 23. Regular Pattern

No. 19. Corbett pattern, craven tan leather, well padded with hair, patent palm grip and patent palm lacing. Set of four gloves, **$3.50**

No. 21. Corbett pattern, dark wine color leather. Well padded with hair and patent palm lacing. Set of four gloves, **$3.00**

No. 23. Regular pattern, fine quality brown tanned leather. A very well made glove. Hair padded and patent palm lacing.
Set of four gloves, **$2.00**

No. 24. Regular pattern, craven tan leather, hair padded, elastic wristband. Set, **$1.50**

SPALDING YOUTHS' BOXING GLOVES
All Styles, Padded with Hair

Spalding Youths' Boxing Gloves are made in exactly the same manner and of the same material as the full size gloves of our manufacture and are warranted to give satisfaction.

No. 45. Youths' Championship Glove, Corbett pattern, best quality brown glove leather, extra well finished and double stitched, patent palm lacing and patent palm grip. Set of four gloves, **$3.50**

No. 40. Youths' size, Corbett pattern, soft craven tan leather, well padded, patent palm lacing. Set of four gloves, **$2.50**

No. 25. Youths' size, regular pattern, soft tanned leather, patent palm lacing. Set of four gloves, **$1.50**

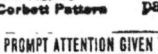

No. 45 Corbett Pattern

No. 25 Regular Pattern

PROMPT ATTENTION GIVEN TO ANY COMMUNICATIONS ADDRESSED TO US — **A. G. SPALDING & BROS.** STORES IN ALL LARGE CITIES — FOR COMPLETE LIST OF STORES SEE INSIDE FRONT COVER OF THIS BOOK

Prices in effect January 5, 1910. Subject to change without notice. • For Canadian prices see special Canadian Catalogue.

THE SPALDING STRIKING BAGS

THE BLADDERS USED IN ALL OUR STRIKING BAGS ARE MADE OF PURE PARA RUBBER (NO COMPOSITION) AND FULLY GUARANTEED

All our single end bags except No. G are made with solid leather top, through center of which rope passes, making them the most certain in action of any. Laces on side at top, so that the bladder can be inflated without interfering with rope. Each bag is most carefully inspected and then packed complete in box with bladder, lace and rope.

No. G

No. G. This is a heavy durable Gymnasium Bag suitable for all around exercise work and the strongest bag made. The cover is of heavy English grain leather, same as used in our best grade foot balls and basket balls and made in the same way. It will outlast two or three bags of any other make. With loop top. . . . . Each, **$8.00**

No. 19. Made of highest quality Patna kid, the lightest and strongest of leather. Sewed with linen thread, double stitched and red welted seams. Especially suited for exhibition work, and a very fast bag. Each, **$7.00**

No. 19S. Same material as No. 19, but furnished with special light bladder and weighs only 7 ounces complete. The fastest bag made, but very strong and durable. . . . . Each, **$7.00**

No. 20. Made of finest selected calfskin, double stitched, red welted seams and reinforced throughout. Very fast and a durable bag for all around use. . . . . Each, **$7.00**

No. 18. The "Fitzsimmons Special." Made of finest selected olive Napa tanned leather, extra well made; double stitched, red welted seams and reinforced throughout. For training purposes particularly this bag will be found extremely satisfactory in every respect. . . . . Each, **$5.00**

No. 18S. Same as No. 18, but smaller in size and lighter. Intended for very speedy work. . . . . Each, **$5.00**

No. 12. Olive tanned leather, specially selected; double stitched, red welted seams and reinforced throughout. Excellent for quick work. Each, **$4.00**

No. 10. Specially tanned brown glove leather; double stitched, red welted seams and reinforced throughout. Very well made. . Each, **$3.50**

No. 17. Made of fine craven tanned leather, well finished; double stitched, red welted seams and reinforced throughout. A good bag. Each, **$3.50**

No. 16. Extra fine grain leather, full size and lined throughout. Each, **3.00**

No. 15. Made of olive tanned leather, full size and lined throughout; red welted seams. . . . . Each, **$2.00**

No. 14. Good quality colored sheepskin; lined throughout. Each, **1.50**

No. 19

SPALDING STRIKING BAG SWIVELS

No. 8   No. 11   No. 9   No. 12   No. 6

No. 8. The simplest and most effective ball bearing swivel on the market. Rope can be changed instantly without interfering with any other part of swivel . Each, **$1.50**

No. 9. With removable socket for quickly suspending or removing bag without readjusting. . . . . . Each, **50c.**

No. 11. Swivel action, with bell cord coupling and rope attached. Fastens permanently to disk; japan finish. . . Each, **50c.**

No. 6. Japanned iron stem for use with platform or disk. . . . . Each, **35c.**

No. 12. Ball and socket action. Fastens permanently to disk; nickel-plated. Each, **25c.**

PROMPT ATTENTION GIVEN TO ANY COMMUNICATIONS ADDRESSED TO US — **A. G. SPALDING & BROS.** STORES IN ALL LARGE CITIES — FOR COMPLETE LIST OF STORES SEE INSIDE FRONT COVER OF THIS BOOK

Prices in effect January 5, 1910. Subject to change without notice. For Canadian prices see special Canadian Catalogue.

THE SPALDING DOUBLE END BAGS

The Bladders used in all our Striking Bags are made of Pure Para Rubber (no composition) and are Fully Guaranteed

We are making all our double end bags with one-piece top and substantial leather loop. Really the strongest construction we know of. The bottom loop is also very strongly made. Each bag complete in box, with bladder, lace, rubber cord for floor, and rope for ceiling attachment.

No. 7. Made of finest selected olive Napa tanned leather and workmanship of same quality as in our "Fitzimmons" Special Bag No. 18. Double stitched, red welted seams. An extremely durable and lively bag. Each, **$5.50**

No. 6. Fine olive tanned leather cover, double stitched, red welted seams. Extra well made throughout. Each, **$5.00**

No. 5. Regulation size, specially tanned brown glove leather cover, red welted seams, double stitched and substantially made throughout. Each, **$4.00**

No. 4½. Regulation size, fine craven tanned leather and red welted seams. Well finished throughout. Each, **$3.75**

No. 4. Regulation size, fine grain leather cover and well made throughout, double stitched. Each, **$3.50**

No. 3. Regulation size, substantial brown leather cover, reinforced and double stitched seams. Each, **$2.50**

No. 2½. Regulation size, good quality dark olive tanned leather, lined throughout, red welted seams. Each, **$2.00**

No. 2. Medium size, good colored sheepskin, lined throughout. Each, **$1.50**

Spalding Bladders

It is well to specify when ordering extra bladders whether they are required for single or double end bags, as we can furnish the two styles in each grade.

Style for Double End Bags and No. 6. Style for Single End Bags.

No. B. With top stem, for Nos. 2, 2½ and 3. Each, **75c.**
No. BS. With side stem, for Nos. 14 and 15. Each, **75c.**
No. 5. With top stem, for Nos. 4, 4½, 5 and 6. Each, **$1.00**
No. 5S. With side stem, for Nos. 10, 12, 16 and 17. Each, **$1.00**
No. 7S. With side stem, for Nos. 18, 18S, 19, 19S and 20. Each, **$1.20**
No. 7. With top stem, for No. 7. **1.20**
No. OM. Top stem for No. G. **1.50**
No. OS. With top stem, heavy bladder, best quality. Each, **$1.25**
No. D. Elastic floor attachment for all double end bags, best quality cord. Each, **30c.**
No. E. Elastic cord for double end bags. Each, **20c.**

Spalding Brass Inflaters

No. 2. Club size, cylinder 10 in. Each, **50c.**
No. 3. Pocket size, cylinder 5⅛ in. **25c.**

All Rubber Bladders bearing our Trade-Mark are made of Pure Para Rubber (no composition) and are guaranteed Perfect in Material and Workmanship. Note special explanation of guarantee on tag attached to each bladder.

Spalding Striking Bag Mitts

No. 1   No. 4   No. 5

Will protect the hands and recommended for use with all Striking Bags.

No. 1. Made of olive Napa Leather and extra well padded; ventilated palm and special elastic wrist in glove. Pair, **$2.50**
No. 2. Made of soft tanned leather, properly shaped and padded, substantially put together. Pair, **$1.50**
No. 3. Made of soft tanned leather, padded and well made; also made in ladies' size. Pair, **75c.**
No. 4. Knuckle mitt, well padded. " **50c.**
No. 5. Knuckle mitt, well padded. " **25c.**

PROMPT ATTENTION GIVEN TO ANY COMMUNICATIONS ADDRESSED TO US

A. G. SPALDING & BROS.
STORES IN ALL LARGE CITIES

FOR COMPLETE LIST OF STORES SEE INSIDE FRONT COVER OF THIS BOOK

Prices in effect January 5, 1910. Subject to change without notice. For Canadian prices see special Canadian Catalogue.

ACCEPT NO SUBSTITUTE THE SPALDING TRADE-MARK **GUARANTEES QUALITY**

The Spalding Disk Platform

Bag is NOT Included with this Platform

Home Apparatus

"Many forms of exercise are indulged in by folk desirous of improving their physical condition, but none of them is more attractive and at the same time more beneficial than bag punching. Arms, shoulders, hands, wrist, the neck and legs are brought into play individually and in combination in bag punching. Aside from the development in these parts of the body, the shoulders are made square and upright, the chest is broadened, the eye quickened and the brain stimulated. The direct result is a new being for the bag puncher."—*Extract from Spalding's Athletic Library, No. 191, "Bag Punching."*

Can be put up in a very small space and taken down quickly when not in use by simply detaching the pipe fixture from the wall plate.

The metal disk against which the bag strikes constitutes one of the best features ever incorporated in an arrangement of this character, rendering it almost noiseless and very quick in action.

This disk also combines an adjustable feature that is simple to operate and makes it possible for various members of the family to use the same disk.

The Spalding Adjustable Disk Platform, without bag.
No. PR. Each, **$5.00**

Patented April 19, 1904

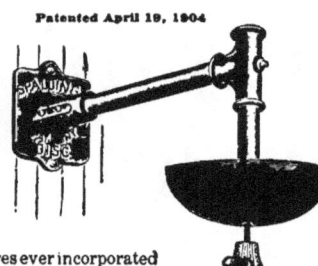

The Spalding Patent Solid Striking Bag Disks

Bag is NOT Included With Either of These Disks

Patent Pending

A striking bag disk must be substantial if it is to be of use, and in the various styles, both adjustable and braced, which we list, this feature has not been neglected, while we have striven to put out a disk which is suitable for home use and moderate in price.

Wall Braced Style

Adjustable Style

No. **FR.** Complete, **Without Bag.** Each, **$5.00**   No. **CR.** Complete, **Without Bag.** Each, **$7.50**

PROMPT ATTENTION GIVEN TO ANY COMMUNICATIONS ADDRESSED TO US   **A. G. SPALDING & BROS.**   **STORES IN ALL LARGE CITIES**   **FOR COMPLETE LIST OF STORES SEE INSIDE FRONT COVER OF THIS BOOK**

Prices in effect January 5, 1910. Subject to change without notice. For Canadian prices see special Canadian Catalogue.

SPALDING'S ATHLETIC LIBRARY
GROUP XII. No. 331.

Schoolyard Athletics

By J. E. SULLIVAN

President Amateur Athletic Union;
Member Board of Education Greater New York.

THE great interest in athletics that has developed in the public schools within recent years has led to the compilation of this book with a view to the systemization of the various events that form the distinctively athletic feature of school recreation. With its aid any teacher should be able to conduct a successful meet, while the directions given for becoming expert in the various lines will appeal to the pupil. Some of the leading athletes have contributed chapters on their specialties: Ray Ewry, holder of the world's high jump record, tells how to practice for that event; Harry Hillman, holder of the hurdle and three-legged records, gives hints on hurdle racing and three-legged racing; Martin Sheridan, all-around champion of America, gives directions for putting the shot; Harry F. Porter, high jump expert, describes how to become proficient in that event. The book is illustrated with photos taken especially for it in public school yards.

PRICE 10 CENTS

ACCEPT NO SUBSTITUTE — THE SPALDING TRADE-MARK **GUARANTEES QUALITY**

Spalding "Official National League" Ball

REG. U. S. PAT. OFF.

Official Ball of the Game for over Thirty Years

 DOPTED by the National League in 1878, and the only ball used in Championship games since that time. Each ball wrapped in tinfoil, packed in a separate box, and sealed in accordance with the latest League regulations. Warranted to last a full game when used under ordinary conditions.

No. 1. Each, $1.25

Per Dozen, $15.00

PROMPT ATTENTION GIVEN TO ANY COMMUNICATIONS ADDRESSED TO US — A. G. SPALDING & BROS. STORES IN ALL LARGE CITIES — **FOR COMPLETE LIST OF STORES SEE INSIDE FRONT COVER OF THIS BOOK**

Prices in effect January 5, 1910. Subject to change without notice. For Canadian prices see special Canadian Catalogue.

ACCEPT NO SUBSTITUTE THE SPALDING TRADE-MARK **GUARANTEES QUALITY**

Durand-Steel Lockers

Wooden lockers are objectionable, because they attract vermin, absorb odors, can be easily broken into, and are dangerous on account of fire.

Lockers made from wire mesh or expanded metal afford little security, as they can be easily entered with wire cutters. Clothes placed in them become covered with dust, and the lockers themselves present a poor appearance, resembling animal cages.

Durand-Steel Lockers are made of finest grade furniture steel and are finished with gloss black, furnace-baked japan (400°), comparable to that used on hospital ware, which will never flake off nor require refinishing, as do paints and enamels.

Some of the 6,000 Durand-Steel Lockers Installed in the Public Gymnasiums of Chicago. 12"x 15"x 42", Double Tier.

Durand-Steel Lockers are usually built with doors perforated full length in panel design with sides and backs solid. This prevents clothes in one locker from coming in contact with wet garments in adjoining lockers, while plenty of ventilation is secured by having the door perforated its entire length, but, if the purchaser prefers, we perforate the backs also.

The cost of Durand-Steel Lockers is no more than that of first-class wooden lockers, and they last as long as the building, are sanitary, secure, and, in addition, are fire-proof.

THE FOLLOWING STANDARD SIZES ARE THOSE MOST COMMONLY USED:

DOUBLE TIER	SINGLE TIER
12 x 12 x 36 Inch	12 x 12 x 60 Inch
15 x 15 x 36 Inch	15 x 15 x 60 Inch
12 x 12 x 42 Inch	12 x 12 x 72 Inch
15 x 15 x 42 Inch	15 x 15 x 72 Inch

SPECIAL SIZES MADE TO ORDER.

We are handling lockers as a special contract business, and shipment will in every case be made direct from the factory in Chicago. If you will let us know the number of lockers, size and arrangement, we shall be glad to take up, through correspondence, the matter of prices.

Six Lockers in Double Tier

Three Lockers in Single Tier

| PROMPT ATTENTION GIVEN TO ANY COMMUNICATIONS ADDRESSED TO US | **A. G. SPALDING & BROS.** STORES IN ALL LARGE CITIES | FOR COMPLETE LIST OF STORES SEE INSIDE FRONT COVER OF THIS BOOK |

Prices in effect January 5, 1910. Subject to change without notice. For Canadian prices see special Canadian Catalogue.

THE following selection of items from their latest Catalogue will give an idea of the great variety of ATHLETIC GOODS manufactured by A. G. SPALDING & BROS. SEND FOR A FREE COPY.

Archery
Bags—
  Bat
  Cricket
  Striking
  Uniform
Balls—
  Base
  Basket
  Cricket
  Field Hockey
  Foot, College
  Foot, Rugby
  Foot, Soccer
  Golf
  Hand
  Indoor
  Medicine
  Playground
  Squash
  Tennis
  Volley
  Water Polo
Bandages, Elastic
Bathing Suits
Bats—
  Base Ball
  Cricket
Belts
Caps—
  Base Ball
  University
  Water Polo
Chest Weights
Circle, Seven-Foot
Coats, Base Ball
Collars, Swimming
Corks, Running
Covers, Racket
Cricket Goods
Croquet Goods
Discus, Olympic
Dumb Bells
Emblems
Equestrian Polo
Exerciser, Home
Felt Letters
Fencing Sticks
Field Hockey
Flags—
  College
  Foul, Base Ball
  Marking, Golf
Foils, Fencing
Foot Balls—
  Association
  College
  Rugby
Glasses, Base Ball
  Sun
  Automobile

Gloves—
  Base Ball
  Boxing
  Cricket
  Fencing
  Foot Ball
  Golf
  Handball
  Hockey, Ice
  Glove Softener
Goals—
  Basket Ball
  Foot Ball
  Hockey, Ice
Golf Clubs
Golf Counters
Golfette
Gymnasium, Home
Gymnasium Board
Hammers, Athletic
Hats, University
Head Harness
Health Pull
Hockey Sticks, Ice
Hole Cutter, Golf
Hole Rim, Golf
Horse, Vaulting
Hurdles, Safety
Hurley Goods
Indian Clubs
Jackets—
  Fencing
  Foot Ball
Javelins
Jerseys
Knee Protectors
Lacrosse
Lanes for Sprints
Lawn Bowls
Leg Guards—
  Base Ball
  Cricket
  Foot Ball
Markers, Tennis
Masks—
  Base Ball
  Fencing
  Nose [inal
Masseur, Abdom-
Mattresses
Megaphones
Mitts—
  Base Ball
  Handball
  Striking Bag
  Moccasins
Nets—
  Cricket
  Golf Driving
  Tennis
  Volley Ball

Numbers, Compet-
Pads— [itors'
  Chamois, Fencing
  Foot Ball
  Sliding, Base Ball
Pants—
  Base Ball
  Basket Ball
  Foot Ball, College
  Foot Ball, Rugby
  Hockey, Ice
  Running
Pennants, College
Plates—
  Base Ball Shoe
  Home
  Marking, Tennis
  Pitchers' Box
  Pitchers' Toe
  Teeing, Golf
  Platforms, Striking
    Bag
Poles—
  Vaulting
  Polo, Roller, Goods
Posts—
  Backstop, Tennis
  Lawn Tennis
Protectors—
  Abdomen
  Base Ball Body
  Eye Glass
Push Ball
Quoits
Rackets, Tennis
Rings—
  Exercising
  Swinging
Rowing Machines
Roque
Sacks, for Sack
  Racing
Score Board, Golf
Score Books—
Score Tablets, Base
Shirts— [Ball
  Athletic
  Base Ball
Shoes—
  Base Ball
  Basket Ball
  Bowling
  Clog
  Cross Country
  Cricket
  Fencing [ation
  Foot Ball, Associ-
  Foot Ball, College
  Foot Ball, Rugby
  Foot Ball, Soccer
  Golf
  Gymnasium

Shoes—
  Jumping
  Running
  Skating
  Squash
  Tennis
Shot—
  Athletic
  Indoor
  Massage
Skates—
  Ice
  Roller
Skis
Sleeve, Pitchers
Snow Shoes
Squash Goods
Straps—
  Base Ball
  For Three-
    Legged Race
  Skate
Stockings
Striking Bags
Suits—
  Basket Ball
  Gymnasium
  Gymnasium,
    Ladies'
  Running
  Soccer
  Swimming
  Union Foot
    Ball
Supporters
  Ankle
  Wrist
Suspensories
Sweaters
Tether Tennis
Tights—
  Full
  Wrestling
  Knee
Toboggans
Trapeze
Trunks—
  Bathing
  Velvet
  Worsted
Umpire Indica-
Uniforms [tor
Wands, Calis-
    thenic
Watches, Stop
Water Wings
Weights, 56-lb.
Whitely Exer-
    cisers
Wrestling
  Equipment

Standard Policy

A Standard Quality must be inseparably linked to a Standard Policy.

Without a definite and Standard Mercantile Policy, it is impossible for a manufacturer to long maintain a Standard Quality.

To market his goods through the jobber, a manufacturer must provide a profit for the jobber as well as the retail dealer. To meet these conditions of Dual Profits, the manufacturer is obliged to set a proportionately high list price on his goods to the consumer.

To enable the glib salesman, when booking his orders, to figure out attractive profits to both the jobber and retailer, these high list prices are absolutely essential; but their real purpose will have been served when the manufacturer has secured his order from the jobber, and the jobber has secured his order from the retailer.

However, these deceptive high list prices are not fair to the consumer, who does not, and, in reality, is not ever expected to pay these fancy list prices.

When the season opens for the sale of such goods, with their misleading but alluring high list prices, the retailer begins to realize his responsibilities, and grapples with the situation as best he can, by offering "special discounts," which vary with local trade conditions.

Under this system of merchandising, the profits to both the manufacturer and the jobber are assured; but as there is no stability maintained in the prices to the consumer, the keen competition amongst the local dealers invariably leads to a demoralized cutting of prices by which the profits of the retailer are practically eliminated.

This demoralization always reacts on the manufacturer. The jobber insists on lower, and still lower, prices. The manufacturer, in his turn, meets this demand for the lowering of prices by the only way open to him, viz.: the cheapening and degrading of the quality of his product.

The foregoing conditions became so intolerable that, ten years ago, in 1899, A. G. Spalding & Bros. determined to rectify this demoralization in the Athletic Goods Trade, and inaugurated what has since become known as "The Spalding Policy."

The "Spalding Policy" eliminates the jobber entirely, so far as Spalding Goods are concerned, and the retail dealer secures his supply of Spalding Athletic Goods direct from the manufacturer under a restricted retail price arrangement by which the retail dealer is assured a fair, legitimate and certain profit on all Spalding Athletic Goods, and the consumer is assured a Standard Quality and is protected from imposition.

The "Spalding Policy" is decidedly for the interest and protection of the users of Athletic Goods, and acts in two ways:

    FIRST—The user is assured of genuine Official Standard Athletic Goods, and the same fixed prices to everybody.

    SECOND—As manufacturers, we can proceed with confidence in purchasing at the proper time, the very best raw materials required in the manufacture of our various goods, well ahead of their respective seasons, and this enables us to provide the necessary quantity and absolutely maintain the Spalding Standard of Quality.

All retail dealers handling Spalding Athletic Goods are required to supply consumers at our regular printed catalogue prices—neither more nor less—the same prices that similar goods are sold for in our New York, Chicago and other stores.

All Spalding dealers, as well as users of Spalding Athletic Goods, are treated exactly alike, and no special rebates or discriminations are allowed to anyone.

Positively, nobody; not even officers, managers, salesmen or other employes of A. G. Spalding & Bros., or any of their relatives or personal friends, can buy Spalding Athletic Goods at a discount from the regular catalogue prices.

This, briefly, is the "Spalding Policy," which has already been in successful operation for the past ten years, and will be indefinitely continued.

In other words, "The Spalding Policy" is a "square deal" for everybody.

A. G. SPALDING & BROS.

By *A. G. Spalding*,
PRESIDENT.

Standard Quality

An article that is universally given the appellation **"Standard"** is thereby conceded to be the Criterion, to which are compared all other things of a similar nature. For instance, the Gold Dollar of the United States is the Standard unit of currency, because it must legally contain a specific proportion of pure gold, and the fact of its being Genuine is **guaranteed** by the Government Stamp thereon. As a protection to the users of this currency against counterfeiting and other tricks, considerable money is expended in maintaining a Secret Service Bureau of Experts. Under the law, citizen manufacturers must depend to a great extent upon Trade-Marks and similar devices to protect themselves against counterfeit products—without the aid of "Government Detectives" or "Public Opinion" to assist them.

Consequently the "Consumer's Protection" against misrepresentation and "inferior quality" rests entirely upon the integrity and responsibility of the "Manufacturer."

A. G. Spalding & Bros. have, by their rigorous attention to "Quality," for thirty-three years, caused their Trade-Mark to become known throughout the world as a Guarantee of Quality as dependable in their field as the U. S. Currency is in its field.

The necessity of upholding the guarantee of the Spalding Trade-Mark and maintaining the Standard Quality of their Athletic Goods, is, therefore, as obvious as is the necessity of the Government in maintaining a Standard Currency.

Thus each consumer is not only insuring himself but also protecting other consumers when he assists a Reliable Manufacturer in upholding his Trade-Mark and all that it stands for. Therefore, we urge all users of our Athletic Goods to assist us in maintaining the Spalding Standard of Excellence, by insisting that our Trade-Mark be plainly stamped on all athletic goods which they buy, because without this precaution our best efforts towards maintaining Standard Quality and preventing fraudulent substitution will be ineffectual.

Manufacturers of Standard Articles invariably suffer the reputation of being high-priced, and this sentiment is fostered and emphasized by makers of "inferior goods," with whom low prices are the main consideration.

A manufacturer of recognized Standard Goods, with a reputation to uphold and a guarantee to protect, must necessarily have higher prices than a manufacturer of cheap goods, whose idea of and basis for a claim for Standard Quality depends principally upon the eloquence of the salesman.

We know from experience that there is no quicksand more **unstable than poverty in quality**—and we avoid this quicksand by Standard Quality.

A. G. Spalding & Bros.

www.ingramcontent.com/pod-product-compliance
Lightning Source LLC
Chambersburg PA
CBHW022117090426
42743CB00008B/889